Telling the Success Story

SUNY Series in Speech Communication
Dudley D. Cahn, Jr., Editor

Telling the Success Story

Acclaiming
and Disclaiming
Discourse

PAMELA J. BENOIT

State University of
New York Press

Published by
State University of New York Press

© 1997 State University of New York

For information, address the State University of New York Press,
State University Plaza, Albany, NY 12246

Production by Bernadine Dawes • Marketing by Fran Keneston

Library of Congress Cataloging-in-Publication Data

Benoit, Pamela J., 1954–
    Telling the success story : acclaiming and disclaiming discourse /
Pamela J. Benoit.
        p.   cm. — (SUNY series in speech communication)
    Includes bibliographical references and index.
    ISBN 0-7914-3317-X (hardcover : alk. paper). — ISBN 0-7914-3318-8
(pbk. : alk. paper)
    1. Self-presentation. 2. Interpersonal communication. 3. Success
in business. I. Title. II. Series.
BF697.5.S44B46 1997
153.6—dc21   96-47391
                                                              CIP

1 2 3 4 5 6 7 8 9 10

Contents

Preface

Self-presentations of success occur in the acceptance addresses of Academy award winners, President Clinton's attempts to take credit for improving economic conditions, corporations' annual reports to stockholders, autobiographies, and the press releases from NASA after Hubble was repaired and started to transmit clear pictures. There are also the stories my daughter tells about figuring out proofs in geometry, the experiences of my colleague who managed to meet a publication deadline, and the narratives of graduate students after they receive a job offer.

While self-presentations are fundamental to the negotiation of identities and affect relational outcomes, they have not received the attention of communication scholars. The purpose of this book is to describe the discursive strategies of success stories as a form of self-presentation. I chose to analyze the success stories of Nobel Prize winners, athletes, and Mary Kay distributors. Nobel Prize winners tell their success stories in acceptance addresses. This case was interesting because the award is well known and the ultimate form of recognition. The pervasiveness of sports in our culture (and in our living rooms) made the success stories of athletes an attractive case for analysis. I realized after completing these two analyses that my tellers were predominantly men so I began to search for a context in which women told their success stories. I found the discourse of Mary Kay distributors at weekly success meetings fascinating and appropriate to my purpose. The women of "Cathy's Comets," the group I observed for five months, were gracious and I appreciate their willingness to let me observe meetings and interview them about their successes. These three cases were engaging and varied contexts for examining success stories.

The publication of this book represents a personal achievement, and I find myself quite self-conscious as I make use of the same strategies I describe in the book. I see this book as an opportunity to expose a fruitful subject for interpersonal scholars rather than an exhaustive theoretical treatment of self-presentation. I think the book lays the foundation for a promising line of inquiry.

I would like to thank Dudley Cahn, the series editor, for his advice and encouragement as well as the anonymous reviewers of the manuscript. At SUNY Press, Priscilla Ross, Jennie Doling, Bernadine Dawes, and Fran Keneston were generous with their assistance and patience. I would also like to thank copyeditor Maria den Boer. Barbara O'Keefe continues to be my role model. She first introduced me to qualitative methods and taught me to ask interesting questions. Mary Jeanette Smythe gave me the time I needed to finish this book and has been an important mentor. Michael Kramer and Stuart Palonsky read versions of chapters and offered helpful suggestions and examples. Many of my graduate students were supportive but special thanks are reserved for Sue Hinton who read field notes, drafts, and entered codes in ETHNOGRAPH for the Mary Kay chapters. My parents believed I could do anything, my brother tutored me on the finer points of golf and baseball for the chapter on sports, and my sister managed to be supportive even when her own life was chaotic. My husband, Bill, read many drafts and was an invaluable editor (and friendly critic) while Jennifer cheerfully endured having a "maniac" for a mother temporarily.

1

Self-Presentation and the Success Story

Success and success stories are cultural preoccupations. Corporate deals, medical advances, peace treaties, Academy Awards, elections and the passage of bills, Man of the Year, movie grosses and Nielsen ratings, *Forbes'* list of the world's richest, my sister's new free-lance job, my advisee's dissertation defense, my daughter's superior rating at her piano competition, and my neighbor's "best yard" award are the substance of success stories. How do individuals tell their own success stories when they want self-praise to stick but they also want to avoid an impression of arrogance?

Self-presentations are fundamental to interpersonal communication. Individuals construe and negotiate their identities with others and give meaning to their discursive behaviors. Relational outcomes, like social approval, are contingent on self-presentations. The self-presentation of a personal success is a particularly exquisite interpersonal accomplishment. The creation and negotiation of a successful identity is poised within competing goals of self-enhancement and modesty.

Beyond Goffman's (1959) *The Presentation of Self in Everyday Life*, self-presentations have not received the attention they deserve from interpersonal scholars because the relevant literature is diverse and disconnected. Accounts, self-descriptions, attribution theory, multiple goals, and narrative are woven together in this book to provide a framework for conceptualizing self-presentations of success. Research undertaken from within the traditions of discourse analysis, rhetorical criticism, communication theory, and social psychology is reviewed and integrated.

Within the literature on self-presentation, image restoration through accounts has received considerable attention. These defensive self-presentations take the form of excuses and justifications to salvage a damaged identity after an undesirable event. The related phenomena of acclaiming a desirable event, like a personal success, has been neglected. This book is unique in its attention to the discursive strategies for acclaiming.

The purpose of this book is to describe the discursive strategies of success stories. The strategies are inductively derived from the texts of three case studies. The analysis is dependent on the data rather than a priori theories. In each case, a qualitative analysis with the constant comparison method is used to generate a typology of acclaiming and disclaiming (i.e., modesty) strategies. The last chapter highlights the progression of this analysis through the cases and considers contextual variations in the discursive strategies for telling a success story.

The goal of this inquiry is consistent with Bochner's (1985) identification of interpretation and intelligibility as a goal of research. This goal is accomplished by developing a typology of discursive strategies for telling success stories and displaying the complexity of this accomplishment by exploring the influence of multiple goals and situations in shaping the discourse. In this book, I have not attempted to predict the effects of these strategies or offer a critical analysis of the discourse. While these are legitimate goals of inquiry (Bochner, 1985), I believe research is most productive when there is a secure foundation based on systematic description.

This first chapter describes the nature of success, reviews the relevant literature on self-presentation and storytelling, and explains the selection of the three case studies that will be used to systematically examine the discursive strategies of success stories. I begin by considering the meaning of success.

THE NATURE OF SUCCESS

Contemplating the nature of success requires consideration of the meaning of success and the social construction of success. Success is often equated with affluence (Biggart, 1983; Cawelti, 1967; Chenoweth, 1974; Goldstein & Smucker, 1986; Huber, 1971; Long, 1981; Wyllie, 1954), but this definition is limited to a single aspect of success. I articulate a broader definition of success that positions the audience as central in identifying and recognizing an individual's success.

DEFINING SUCCESS

We know success when we see it, but what do we mean by it? Dictionaries focus on fame, rank, and prosperity as indicators of success and specify that success occurs when a planned outcome is achieved. I would elaborate on this definition to incorporate the idea that a successful behavior is one that is distinctive and desirable.[1]

Distinctiveness sets an individual's behavior apart from the crowd by having done the action first, bigger, longer, farther, faster, or better than others. Inherently, distinctiveness involves a comparison and elevates some individuals for their accomplishments. Neil Armstrong first stepped on the moon (Carruth, 1991). Ellen Futter, appointed to lead Barnard College at the age of 31, was the youngest person to assume the post of a college president (Guinness Multimedia, 1995). The first person to scale the world's three highest mountains was Reinhold Messner (Guinness Multimedia, 1995). Steven Spielberg's films account for seven of the top ten grossing movies, generating more than $2 billion (Guinness Multimedia, 1995). Each of these individuals have been judged successes for completing a distinctive act.

But distinctiveness is not sufficient for an act to be considered a success, for the behavior must also be regarded as desirable to the salient audience. Although variations occur, acts within a Western culture are generally judged favorably if they (1) improve the human condition, (2) represent control over mind/body, or (3) secure valued rewards.

Technological advances, medical discoveries, and great literature and art can be judged successful endeavors because individual actions produce outcomes that enrich the human existence. Engineers at Digital Equipment Corporation have produced the fastest computer microprocessor, contributing to the advance of information technology (Guinness Multimedia, 1995). Recently, a team of scientists discovered a gene linked to Alzheimer's disease. The discovery was proclaimed a "kind of a Holy Grail," with implications for millions suffering from the disease ("Gene Find," 1995, p. 7A). Maya Angelou's poetry and autobiography are literary contributions that voice the essence of humanity (Phillip, 1995). The actions of some individuals are noteworthy because they can be perceived as improving the quality of human life.

Behaviors demonstrating control over the mind or body are also considered worthy of recognition. The creative act, intellectual breakthrough, personal transformation, and peak athletic performance are recognized as praiseworthy. The recent intellectual discovery that a statue of Cupid is a missing Michelangelo is a success for art historian Kathleen Weil-Garris Brandt ("Lucky Find?" 1996). Mark Rypien's 30-yard pass to Gary Clark in the third quarter of Super Bowl XXVI was executed perfectly, preventing a comeback by the Buffalo Bills ("Rypien's Truth," 1992). The perfection of pianist Andre Watts' concerts have generated tremendous acclaim (Oestreich, 1995). The process of mastering mind and body in creating favorable outcomes is evidence of a personal success.

Behaviors are symbolically linked to success when they are instrumental in obtaining valued rewards (e.g., status, wealth, prestige). The possession of these rewards are indicators of success. In this culture, money is a cardinal symbol of success, and *Forbes* magazine's list of the world's richest individuals identifies the most successful persons. Bill Gates of Microsoft Corporation led the list in 1995 with a $12.9 billion fortune ("Rolling in Dough," 1995). Former President Jimmy Carter has earned considerable prestige by serving as an unofficial negotiator in international conflict (Nelan, 1994). Colin Powell held the rank of a four-star general and the position of the chairman of the Joint Chiefs of Staff before his retirement in 1993 ("Retired, Colin Powell," 1993). His rank and importance as a military advisor fueled interest in his book and a possible presidential bid. Each of these individuals can claim they are a success.

SUCCESS AS A SOCIAL CONSTRUCT

It is important for individuals to succeed. Success may be attained by becoming a wealthy businessperson, winning basketball games, making good grades, or being elected to political office. Success/achievement is consistently identified as a basic value in Western culture (Rokeach, 1973; Steele & Redding, 1962) and a primary motivating influence for human behavior (Herzberg, 1959; Maslow, 1970). Whoever a person is or however that person acts, it is imperative to be recognized and appreciated as successful.

Notwithstanding its importance to individuals, success is also essential to social order. Societies promote specific behaviors by recognizing them as achievements worthy of praise/rewards and deter others through punishments (Jellison, 1990; Kanouse, Gumpert, & Canavan-Gumpert, 1981). Jellison (1990) notes: "Each social group designates some behaviors as desirable and others as undesirable. While the content of such lists of positive and negative actions varies from one group to another, every society seems to make such distinctions" (p. 285). A culture's values are communicated by what behaviors count as achievements. Success is thus socially construed because it is dependent on the values of a social group. Praise of others provides "an important mechanism for the social transmission of values. Every statement of praise contains some information—though not always explicitly—about what is and is not valued" (Goode, 1978, p. 101).

The audience is central to recognizing and rewarding success. An individual's claim to success must be accepted by others to receive the desired recognition. We are pleased when others praise our achievements and irritated when they fail to credit our efforts. This dependence on external evaluations is rooted in Western religious and political ideologies that repress the intrinsic merit of the individual and locate self-worth in the evaluations of external identities (Baumeister, 1982). An achievement is ultimately most satisfying when it has been credited in public. Consequently, the audience for a successful performance assumes a prominent role in defining the behavior as a success and determining the appropriate recognition (D'Arcy, 1963), motivating individuals to shape the impressions others form of their behaviors and identities by telling their own success stories.

Individuals seek recognition for behavior that others judge as successful to validate their self-worth, while societies control and motivate members by selecting particular behaviors to value. Distinctive and desirable behaviors are perceived as successful, but the meaning attributed to a behavior is negotiable. Will a behavior be viewed as an important success? Will the individual be seen as responsible for the behavior? Because success is socially construed, individuals are motivated to shape other's impressions through self-presentations.

SELF-PRESENTATION

A self-presentation projects an individual's identity or image before an audience.[2] These self-presentations may involve defensive or assertive impression management (Bromley, 1993; Tedeschi & Norman, 1985). Defensive impression management repairs a tarnished identity. Actions with perceived negative consequences are likely to generate discursive accounts directed toward relevant audiences (Baaten, Cody, & DeTienne, 1993; Schönbach, 1980, 1990; Scott & Lyman, 1968). Hugh Grant's arrest for soliciting a prostitute was followed by defensive impression management. In his account, Grant repeatedly took responsibility and apologized for his actions (Corliss, 1995). Assertive impression management entails a self-presentation of positive qualities, attributes, and behaviors. Bob Dole's (1996) homepage on the World Wide Web includes a personal message that involves assertive impression management: "To be a great President requires unique qualities of character, experience and leadership. In my life, I've been tested in many ways and have always found strength in the values that make this country great: faith in God, belief in community, personal responsibility and love of family." This statement suggests that Bob Dole has acquired favorable attributes by overcoming difficult challenges. His self-presentation acclaims his positive identity as a compelling reason for supporting him for president. This discourse is enacted to accomplish the goal of creating a positive identity.[3]

To elaborate on self-presentation, this discussion must start by considering the underlying motives for self-presentation. Then the literature on defensive self-presentation will be briefly reviewed as a contrast to the last section on assertive self-presentations.

MOTIVES FOR SELF-PRESENTATION

To understand why we engage in self-presentation, theorists have identified four primary motives: (1) self-esteem, (2) identity development, (3) social and material rewards, and (4) social approval. A self-presentation can enhance an individual's sense of self-worth. A football player who recounts his role in the championship game relives the moment and confirms his importance to the team and himself. This fundamental motive involves seeking respect and honor to enhance self-esteem.

A self-presentation can assist in the development of a self-identity. Self-descriptions are ways of coming to know who we are and what attributes can be claimed. Sarah lands a fantastic job in sales and calls her friends. Her story about how she managed to get this job reinforces her positive evaluation of her own abilities, and Sarah comes to see herself as possessing qualities consistent with a successful interview and a desirable position in sales. In this sense, telling the story is a way of making it (the success) so.

Social exchange theorists situate motive in the desire to receive rewards and avoid punishments (Reis & Gruzen, 1976; Roloff, 1981; Thibaut & Kelley, 1978). Presenting a favorable identity increases the probability of receiving rewards from others. Frank negotiates an important merger for his company. At the next staff meeting, he describes his efforts and his boss is convinced Frank was instrumental in the deal. He gets a promotion. Frank secures increased status and power through his negotiating and self-presentational skills.

The final motive for self-presentation is social approval (Arkin, 1980; Arkin & Shepperd, 1990; Baumeister, 1982; Jellison & Gentry, 1978; Tetlock & Manstead, 1985). By creating an impression that will be positively assessed, individuals can receive the favor of others (Baumeister, 1982; Kauffman & Skiner, 1968; Leary & Kowalski, 1990; Schlenker, 1982). Social approval plays a central role in human behavior as an instrumental goal (Arkin, 1980; Jellison & Gentry, 1978; Jones, 1964), mediating a variety of other desired rewards like material goods, friendship, power, and self-esteem. A new acquaintance may create an impression of similarity, optimism, and affability to promote social approval. That approval may generate rewards in the form of liking and admiration from an interactional partner.

The four motives for self-presentation (self-esteem, identity development, social and material rewards, social approval) are often interrelated. Creating an impression of competence in an interview could lead to material rewards (e.g., salary) and simultaneously enhance the self-esteem of the job candidate. Individuals who acquire social approval through self-presentation are also likely to be given material and social rewards. While the motives may be complicated and entangled in any given situation, it is clear that there are compelling reasons to engage in self-presentation.

DEFENSIVE SELF-PRESENTATIONS: ACCOUNTS

When an individual's image is damaged, accounts are the discursive self-presentations designed to manage the predicament.[4] Typologies of account strategies focus on excuses and justifications (Benoit, 1995; Bromley, 1993; D'Arcy, 1963; Goffman, 1971; Schlenker, 1980; Schönbach, 1980, 1990; Scott & Lyman, 1968; Semin & Manstead, 1983; Snyder, Higgins, & Stucky, 1983; Sykes & Matza, 1957; Tedeschi & Riess, 1981b). Excuses minimize responsibility but admit the behavior is negative (e.g., "I insulted you but I was drunk at the time"). Justifications accept responsibility but minimize the negative consequences (e.g., "I ran a red light but no one got hurt").

Accounts are relevant to acclaims because explanations for failure events provide a contrast to the explications of success events. Acclaims take credit for a desirable event while accounts avoid blame for an undesirable event. Both accounts and acclaims deal with responsibility for an act and the evaluation of an act. Excuses deny or minimize responsibility for the negative act, while an interactant who acclaims a success seeks to secure or maximize responsibility for a positive act. Similarly, justifications reduce the negativity of the event, while acclaims heighten the positivity of the act.

ASSERTIVE SELF-PRESENTATIONS

Unlike defensive impression management, assertive self-presentations project favorable identities (e.g., competence, likeable, successful). The strategies identified in the literature, and reviewed here, for establishing a positive image include nonverbal behaviors, positive association, rendering favors, opinion conformity, compliments, and self-enhancement.

Nonverbal Behavior

Schlenker (1980) and DePaulo (1992) reexamined smiling, eye contact, body language, space, and paralanguage as self-presentational strategies. For example, in one line of research, investigators have isolated nonverbal behaviors associated with an aggressive communication style. In situations like job interviews, aggressiveness may create the impression of confidence and ability. In Dipboye and Wiley's (1977) study, recruiters viewed job candidates who were either moderately aggressive or passive. A moderately aggressive candidate appeared confident, demonstrated good eye contact, spoke forcefully, and answered questions at length, while a passive candidate appeared tense and shy, exhibited poor eye contact, spoke softly, and gave abbreviated answers to questions. Moderately aggressive job candidates were rated more favorably by recruiters. In a second study (Dipboye & Wiley, 1978), participants assuming the role of a college recruiter were also more likely to recommend hiring candidates who used an aggressive style. Not surprisingly, this cluster of moderately aggressive communication behaviors is associated with a positive impression in a situation where judgments of competence are central to the evaluation and the motivation to present a favorable identity is elevated. Nonverbal behaviors appear rich and complex in conveying immediacy, positive affect, power, and competence.

Positive Association

An indirect form of self-presentation occurs when an individual claims a connection to other people, objects, or events that are positively valued. Cialdini's classic work on basking in reflected glory (BIRG) suggests that individuals generalize positive evaluations of others even when there is a superficial connection to themselves. When participants in Cialdini's (1989) study believed they shared a birthday with a famous person, they typically revealed this information to people they wanted to impress. When the football team won, college students wore more university apparel than when they lost (Cialdini, Borden, Thorne, Walker, Freeman, & Sloan, 1976). I've noticed that on my campus, students wear more university apparel during basketball season than football season reflecting the teams' respective records. The positive association reflects on the individual claiming a connection to persons/institutions already evaluated favorably (Bromley, 1993).

Rendering Favors

Self-presenters render favors because persons who do nice things are typically liked (Jones, 1964; Jones & Pittman, 1980; Jones & Wortman, 1973). After a long day at work, I came home to find that my daughter had fixed dinner. This favor created a self-presentation emphasizing her thoughtfulness. Favors may establish reciprocity with the other person to secure some future reward (Gouldner, 1960; Tedeschi & Melburg, 1984). I remembered that my daughter had been thoughtful when she asked me to drive her to the mall a couple of days later. Favors are more likely to be appreciated and reciprocated when the favor is valued by the recipient, does not compromise the recipient's future behavior, and involves sacrifice on the part of the granter (Brehm & Cole, 1966; Muir & Weinstein, 1962; Tesser, Gatewood, & Driver, 1968). The intentions of the favor granter are evaluated by recipients. But if ulterior motives are perceived, the impression will not be positive (Schopler & Thompson, 1968).

Opinion Conformity

The relationship between liking and similarity of opinions is well documented (Berscheid & Walster, 1978; Bryne, 1961, 1971). Liked individuals are perceived as intelligent, competent, and adjusted (Bryne, 1971). We may be more attracted to those who share our beliefs because they reinforce our own judgments, facilitate smooth interactions and cooperation in achieving goals, and establish reciprocity of liking (Ralston & Elsass, 1991; Wortman & Linsenmeier, 1977). Expressing a similar opinion can create a favorable identity with an audience.

Individuals dependent on others for rewards are more likely to conform (Davis & Florquist, 1965; Jones, 1965) to secure those rewards. Because the job interview is overtly self-presentational, research has investigated the role of opinion conformity in this context. Job candidates who express more similarity with interviewers are seen as more competent and worthier of a recommendation than those who conform less (Baskett, 1973).

Consider another self-presentational situation: Mark introduces his new girlfriend to his best friend. The girlfriend wants Mark's best friend to like her. During the course of a conversation, she agrees that Dallas will win the Super Bowl and that Sociology 120 is a stupid class. This similarity of opinions leads to extended conversation and the best friend's belief that Mark has a terrific girlfriend. The interaction is enjoyable, the best friend's attitudes are reinforced, and a basis for reciprocity of liking has been established.[5]

But the self-presenter must avoid being perceived as excessively dependent or ingratiating. Jones, Jones, and Gergen (1963) found that individuals who were seen as dependent on their partner and agreed continually were liked less and seen as more ingratiating than those who agreed intermittently. The organizational literature suggests self-presenters can use the strategy of yielding, expressing initial disagreement before acquiescing later in an interaction (Wortman & Linsenmeier, 1977). The presumed advantage of this strategy is that it obtains the rewards of conformity without the appearance of ingratiation.

Compliments

Compliments are self-presentation strategies that create a respectful and generous identity. It makes intuitive sense that those who give compliments are liked by those who receive the compliment (Aronson & Linder, 1965; Mette, 1971). Kipnis and Vanderveer (1971) studied the effect of compliments on performance assessments to determine if they were an effective self-presentational strategy. Participants in the role of a supervisor were asked to evaluate workers. One of the average workers gave the supervisor a compliment. The complimenter received the highest performance appraisal even though another worker had actually performed better on the task. This research suggests that the compliment uses a form of self-presentation that led to a positive evaluation by a supervisor.

The effectiveness of compliments as a self-presentation strategy can be influenced by judgments of speaker intent and believability. If the recipient of a compliment suspects an ulterior motive or rejects the accuracy of the compliment, liking does not follow and ingratiation is suspected (Dickoff, 1964; Jones & Schneider, 1968; Regan, 1976). A compliment is most effective when it is perceived as sincere and accurate.

Recently, I overheard a graduate student compliment a professor for remembering the substance of an article that they had discussed several months before. The compliment appeared sincere and accurate and the student was seen by that professor to be attentive and appreciative. The compliment reinforced this professor's positive assessment of the student.

Self-Enhancement

When we tell people about who we are and what qualities we possess, there are opportunities for self-enhancement. These verbal self-promotions can convey a positive identity to an audience (Bromley, 1993). These kinds of statements probably sound familiar: "I'm the first chair in the brass section of the band." "I've been a member of the Million Dollar Roundtable for sales for the last three years." "My best quality is that I'm continually looking for opportunities to grow as a person." "I know my way around a computer." Research consistently documents that individuals routinely offer positive evaluations of their abilities and qualities before audiences (Jones, Gergen, & Jones, 1963; Schlenker, Wiegold, & Hallam, 1990). Individuals present themselves as possessing positive characteristics because "if these self-enhancing communications are persuasive, the source will gain the respect and liking of the target" (Tedeschi & Melburg, 1984, p. 38). Self-presentational goals can be accomplished through self-enhancements.

But audience perceptions of speaker's intentions can influence the effectiveness of the presentation. If the enhancement is perceived as deliberate, individuals are judged as less sociable, competent, emotionally stable, and pleasant (Fletcher, 1990). The interactional context of a self-enhancing remark also influences its interpretation. An interactant whose self-enhancing

remark is in response to a question from an interactional partner is considered more likeable and considerate than a person
who interjects a positive self-description that is not elicited
(Holtgraves & Srull, 1989). Verbal self-descriptions must avoid
the appearance of manipulation and arrogance.

In summary, the literature on assertive self-presentation
includes descriptions of strategies for projecting a favorable
identity and variables that influence the effectiveness of the
strategies with audiences. Nonverbal behaviors, positive association, rendering favors, opinion conformity, compliments, and
self-enhancement are a diverse set of strategies of varying
relevance to acclaiming self-presentations in success stories. Nonverbal behaviors are of less interest to this project on discursive
strategies whereas the literature on self-enhancements is relevant
because acclaiming centers attention on describing the self as
successful. A serious limitation to this work is that it ignores
the nature of the self-enhancing message. The next section
considers research pertaining specifically to self-presentations
of success.

SELF-PRESENTATIONS OF SUCCESS

Attribution theorists, beginning with Heider (1958), have explored
causal explanations for success as well as failure. A self-serving
bias, accepting credit for success and avoiding responsibility for
one's own failure, is well documented (Arkin, Cooper, & Kolditz,
1980; Bradley, 1978; Brown & Gallagher, 1992; House, 1980;
Miller & Ross, 1975; Snyder, Stephan, & Rosenfield, 1978;
Tedeschi & Linkskold, 1976). A self-presentational explanation
for this bias indicates that a success creates a positive identity for
the individual and a self-presentation is offered to "capitalize on
that outcome" (Arkin & Shepperd, 1990, p. 185). A teller of a
success story can influence others to attribute responsibility for a
significant success and thereby realize self-presentational motives.
The literature on self-presentations of success can be divided into
two parts. Acclaiming self-presentations attempt to secure recognition for an important success. Disclaiming self-presentations
attend to modesty in telling the success story.

ACCLAIMING SELF-PRESENTATIONS

Accounts of problematic acts have received considerable attention in the literature compared to acclaims of successful acts. Acclaims are the opposite of accounts. The literature on accounts identifies reduced responsibility for an act (excuses) and the evaluation of an act as less negative (justifications) as dominant issues in the discourse. By extension, acclaims would involve increased responsibility and the positive evaluation of an act as its dominant issues. Entitlements refer to discourse that claims responsibility for a success, and enhancements include discourse that magnifies the desirability of the achievement (Schlenker, 1980; Tedeschi & Melburg, 1984; Tedeschi & Norman, 1985; Tedeschi & Riess, 1981a). Although the literature relevant to acclaiming is limited, it is worth examining studies that pertain to entitlements and enhancements.

Entitlements

> We did it our way baby! We did it! We did it! We did it! [Barry Switzer to Jerry Jones, after Dallas won Super Bowl XXX ("Dallas Defense," 1996, p. 10B)]

> As a result of our efforts, the economy now is on a path of rising output, increasing employment, and falling deficits. [President Clinton, in his first economic report to Congress ("President Brags," 1994, p. 10A)]

Entitlements claim responsibility for a positive outcome. Barry Switzer asserts that he and the owner played an instrumental role in winning an unprecedented third Super Bowl victory in four years for Dallas. President Clinton connects positive economic news to his administration's deficit reduction plan. The teller of a success story is interested in shaping an audience's attributions of responsibility because recognition is reserved for individuals who caused the positive outcome. D'Arcy (1963) observes that "we do not praise an act, however good its nature, if it is done by accident, or by mistake, or through inadvertence, or through circumstances beyond the

agent's control" (p. 125). I would add that praise is not forth-
coming for an individual unless an audience believes that there
is evidence of personal responsibility.

Studies have investigated the effect of an entitlement on
audience perceptions. Giacalone (1985) found that an individual
claiming credit for a medical discovery was rated most favorably
when a third party confirmed that the individual deserved the
credit. An individual was perceived more favorably if that person had to go against the group consensus to make the discovery. Attribution to the group versus the individual is also an
issue in Decker's (1987, 1990) work on perceptions of managers. Managers with individual accomplishments were rated more
favorably than those with successful groups.

Entitlements are designed to shape an audience's perception of responsibility in order to secure recognition for a positive act, but the research on audience perceptions warns tellers
of success stories that their entitlements may be perceived as
boastful. Miller, Cooke, Tsang, and Morgan (1992) investigate
one form of entitlement—attributing an achievement to an
individual's internal disposition—and found that it is consistently perceived as bragging. To entitle or not to entitle? How
to entitle? The intricacy of telling the success story and the
teller's accomplishment is becoming more apparent.

Enhancements

> This treaty is good for all mankind. [President George Bush
> on the eve of a summit to sign a long-range nuclear weapons
> treaty with Russian President Boris Yeltsin ("Summit Set,"
> 1992, p. 1A)]

> My job is to show people they can overcome their problems.
> I feel most aligned with the underdog, and the down-and-
> out, the lost and disenfranchised—those defenseless and those
> afraid. I feel a deep empathy for them. [Ron Kovic, author
> of *Born on the Fourth of July* ("Brash," 1990, p. 4)]

Tellers of success stories attempt to shape perceptions of
the importance of their achievement to increase recognition for

that act. Bush touts the agreement as an unqualified success for his administration. The actions of political leaders, including himself, have made the world a safer place for the rest of us. Ron Kovic enhances the importance of his writing by arguing that it helps others overcome their problems by providing a voice for those who are powerless.

Studies relevant to enhancements have investigated task difficulty, assuming that the more difficult the task, the more important the success. Tedeschi and Riess (1981b) found that skiers see their own successes as more significant by claiming that the race course was difficult. In a study of perceptions of managers, Giacalone and Riordan (1990) found that managers who describe obstacles in completing a project were given more credit than a modest manager. But contrary to expectations, obstacles were not related to assessments of task difficulty and task difficulty did not affect recognition. The authors speculate that recognition is tied to ability rather than effort. This study also revealed interesting gender differences. Women's successes were seen as the product of effort and less deserving of recognition, while men's successes were perceived as the product of ability and more deserving of recognition.[6]

The literature reviewed in this section on entitlements and enhancements primarily concerns effects without considering discursive practices for enacting entitlements and enhancements. As a result, the research is suggestive but fragmentary. By systematically examining the discourse of success stories, a typology of discursive strategies for acclaiming can be developed.

DISCLAIMING SELF-PRESENTATIONS

Tellers must orient to multiple goals in telling their success stories. Tellers who acclaim successes may secure recognition but risk attributions of arrogance and bragging (Decker, 1987; Giacalone, 1985; Miller, Cooke, Tsang, & Morgan, 1992). Tellers who disclaim may appear modest but fail to convince audiences to attribute personal responsibility or value the success.

The literature on multiple goals is a starting point for appreciating disclaiming self-presentations as relevant to success

story discourse. Then, research on modesty versus self-aggrandizement is reviewed and assessed. Finally, a conceptual framework for disclaiming is constructed.

Multiple goals

The foundation for considering the success story as discourse
in which multiple goals are salient is based on prior research
on multiple interactional goals. Brown and Levinson's (1978,
1987) politeness theory significantly advanced our understanding of interactional goals by attending to face issues. But politeness theory concentrates on the face needs of an interactional
partner rather than the face issues of self (Craig, Tracy, &
Spisak, 1986; Tracy, 1990; Tracy & Baratz, 1995), while the
telling of a success story is concerned with the projection of the
teller's positive face. Tracy (1990) argues that politeness theory
has not considered competing face goals. The teller of a success
story wants both to secure recognition and be perceived as
modest to be appreciated.

In intellectual discussions, for example, dilemmas are rooted
in competing identity goals (Tracy & Baratz, 1995). A discus-
sant wants to be perceived as competent but modest, as critical
but supportive:

> A fierce pursuit of another's claim could be seen as support-
> ing intellectual standards and the group goal of advancing
> ideas, or it could be seen as self-aggrandizing intellectual
> display. Gentle, non-threatening questioning could display a
> commitment to community and a concern to not threaten
> another's face, or it could be taken as letting poor scholar-
> ship go by and/or evidencing intellectual limitations of one
> or another party. (Tracy & Baratz, 1995, p. 308)

Trade-offs of goals become impossible to avoid. Multiple goals
are considered a function of situated talk.

Although the literature does not address the particular
multiple goals salient in the telling of success stories, it does
offer a framework for understanding how interactants orient

to competing goals. O'Keefe and Shepherd (1987, 1989) advance three methods for managing instrumental and face goals: selection, separation, and integration. With a selection strategy, an interactant chooses the most important goal and then enacts behaviors appropriate to that goal without giving attention to other goals. A separation strategy allows the interactant to address multiple goals in different parts of the discourse. Interactants redefine the meaning of the behavior and the situation to avoid the trade-offs between competing goals with an integration strategy. O'Keefe (1988, 1991) reasons that differences in goal-management strategies exhibit variations in message design logics.

Research from a conversational analytic tradition circumvents the concept of goals and intentions (Mandlebaum & Pomerantz, 1995; Pomerantz, 1978). Pomerantz (1978) details the multiple constraints faced by a recipient of a compliment. The preference for agreement and the need to avoid self-praise are interactionally managed through a set of discourse solutions. Downgrades "partially satisfy each of the conflicting preferences" (p. 101). Another solution involves referent shifts. By shifting credit away from self, the response "displays a sensitivity to self-praise avoidance" and is "partially supportive of, that is, a partial warrant for or legitimization of, the prior praise" (p. 105). A return compliment functions similarly to agree implicitly with the compliment, but it also shifts attention to others and thereby avoids self-praise. Talk is an interactional accomplishment that attends to competing constraints.

This literature on multiple goals leads to an appreciation of the intricacy and practical accomplishment of an interactant's discourse. Unfortunately, the research comparing modesty and self-aggrandizement is directed entirely toward predicting which goal will be salient rather than balancing or integrating them. This literature is taken up in this next section.

Choosing to Disclaim or Acclaim

Although the question of disclaiming and acclaiming has not been framed in relationship to multiple goals, there has been research that isolates variables influencing the choice between a modest or a self-aggrandizing presentation. Before considering this work, it is important to understand that this research assumes that modesty or bragging is an either/or choice. O'Keefe and Shepherd's (1987, 1989) separation and integration strategies for multiple goals make a convincing argument that interactants have other choices (e.g., both/and, neither). This research also assumes that messages enacting modest and acclaiming self-presentations are equivalent. No attempt is made to investigate the discursive strategies for enacting disclaiming or acclaiming self-presentations. Despite these limitations, the research provides information about audience, source, and event influences on disclaiming.

Audience. The audience influences the interactant's decision to produce a modest identity. If an audience has prior knowledge of an individual's success, a modest presentation is selected (Baumeister & Jones, 1978; Jones & Wortman, 1973; Schlenker, 1980; Schlenker & Leary, 1982), and the presenter is perceived as competent, modest, but less truthful than an individual who acclaims (Schlenker & Leary, 1982). A presenter who expects the audience to be evaluative rather than supportive also chooses to be modest (Schneider, 1969). There is some evidence that interactants take their cue from their partners. If the partner disclaims, then the interactant also presents a modest identity (Gergen & Wishnov, 1965; Schneider & Eustis, 1972), conforming to the implied expectations. An expectation of future interaction induces a modest self-presentation (Eagly & Acksen, 1971; Whitehead & Smith, 1986) because a modest identity is easier to sustain in future interactions.

Source. Source influence studies investigate individual differences as the predictors of modest self-presentations. Self-esteem, feelings of personal control, self-confidence, and social anxiety can reverse a self-serving bias and produce modest self-presentations (Schlenker & Wiegold, 1992; Weary & Arkin, 1981). Schlenker, Wiegold, and Hallam (1990) found that individuals with low self-esteem who were being evaluated by an audience behaved modestly, while high self-esteem subjects were self-enhancing. Similarly, Arkin, Appleman, and Berger (1980) discovered that individuals with high anxiety scores produced modest self-appraisals for an evaluative audience compared to those with low anxiety scores.

Event. The success event can be caused by the actions of an individual or a group. Zaccaro, Peterson, and Walker (1987) examined the attributions made by players of individually oriented sports (e.g., baseball) and group sports that required greater interdependence between players (e.g., football). Individuals were more likely to share credit with the group in sports requiring interdependence (e.g., "The team really worked well together and that's why we got as far as we did"). Although the group's performance is acclaimed, the individual appears modest in sharing credit with others.

At the intersection of audience and the description of the success event are issues of believability. Self-enhancement and modesty are influenced by the plausibility of the success. If a person's story is judged as an unlikely tale, the teller may be marked as an "egotist, irritant, or uncooperative social participant" (Schlenker & Wiegold, 1992, p. 144). Believability, like Fisher's (1987) narrative fidelity, constrains a self-presentation and prompts more modest claims of success.

In predicting the occurrence of modest self-descriptions, the literature considers the variables of audience, source, and event. These variables predict the choice of message without considering the message itself. In the next section, I offer a conceptual framework for disclaiming discourse.

Disclaiming Strategies

Because the essential issues of the success story consider responsibility and evaluation of the act, it follows that disclaiming discourse would also address these issues. Disclaiming discourse could be expected to have counterparts to entitlements and enhancements. These take the form of dissociations and detractions.

Dissociations.

> I had the air-conditioning at my back. [Rusty Friche, after kicking a 60-yard field goal ("They Said It," 1993, p. 16)]

> I have never accepted what many people have kindly said—namely that I inspired the nation. Their will was resolute and remorseless, and as it proved, unconquerable. It fell to me to express it. [Winston Churchill, in his eightieth birthday address to Parliament (Hyman, 1985)]

I designate the complement of an entitlement to be a dissociation. This type of disclaiming discourse reduces the individual's responsibility for the success, lessening the connection between the success and the teller of the success story. Rusty Friche attributes his success to the playing conditions while Winston Churchill declines credit for withstanding Hitler's advances and recognizes the British people. A strategy for enacting dissociation—sharing credit with others (Decker, 1987, 1990; Miller, Cooke, Tsang, & Morgan, 1992)—has been investigated previously and found to be associated with increased ratings of liking and social sensitivity by audiences. Miller, Cooke, Tsang, and Morgan (1992) briefly mention showing honor or gratitude for a recognition as evidence of a modest self-presentation. This strategy would also be consistent with the definition of dissociation because the self-presenter focuses attention on others rather than self.

Detractions.

> I mean, most people work hard for what they do. I spend a lot of time at it. But what do I do? I only play music one hour a night. I don't work 14 hours a day driving a cab. [Harry Connick, Jr., pianist ("Jazzy Harry," 1990, p. 5)]

One never notices what has been done; one can only see what remains to be done. [Marie Curie (Daintith, Egerton, Fergusson, Stibbs, & Wright, 1989)]

Detractions are the counterpart of enhancements. Detractions minimize or downgrade the significance of the success. Harry Connick, Jr. compares the number of hours he actually works to the hours worked by a cab driver to suggest that his achievement is less noteworthy than that of the cab driver. Marie Curie does not dwell on past accomplishments but is concerned with attaining future goals. Her success is incomplete. Detractions, like these examples, are not considered in the literature.

In telling the success story, interactants attempt to accomplish the multiple goals of securing recognition and appearing modest. Their orientation to these competing goals explains the presence of acclaiming and disclaiming discourse in success stories. Acclaiming has been sectioned into entitlements and enhancements, and disclaiming is divided into dissociations and detractions. Although the literature virtually ignores the message itself and is incomplete, it does provide a self-presentational framework for the analysis of discursive strategies of success stories.

THE SUCCESS STORY

Following Gergen and Gergen's (1988) synthesis of definitions and essential features of the concept of story, a success story will be defined as a narrative that interprets a behavior as a success, selects and orders events relating to that success, and includes a causal attribution for the success. Stories are not simply reportings of behaviors and experiences but tellings that interpret their meaning (Bruner, 1990). Rosenwald and Ochberg (1992) argue that "personal stories are not merely a way of telling someone (or oneself) about one's life; they are the means by which identities may be fashioned" (p. 1). They are inherently social events, publicly performed and negotiated (Gergen & Gergen, 1988).

Stories may be accepted or rejected by recipients so that the telling "depends importantly on the individual's ability to negotiate successfully with others concerning the meaning of events in relationship with each other" (Gergen & Gergen, 1988, p. 38). When an individual completes a behavior that could be construed as a success and the audience has knowledge of it, they determine whether to recognize it as a success. If some form of recognition occurs, the teller's success story is implicitly or explicitly elicited. If the recognition does not follow, a teller may attempt to shape the audience's judgment by telling a spontaneous success story. Recipients of success stories may accept or reject them, thus constraining what can be told (Fisher, 1987; Schlenker & Wiegold, 1992).

PURPOSE

The purpose of this book is to describe the discursive strategies of success stories. The stories of Nobel Prize winners, athletes, and Mary Kay distributors are analyzed in the chapters that follow. These case studies were selected for their diversity in domain, tellers, and audiences in an attempt to create a cross-situational explanation of the discursive strategies of success stories.

Chapter 2 presents an analysis of Nobel Prize winners' acceptance addresses. The tellers of these success stories are prominent scientists, authors, and statesmen. Winners of Nobel Prizes are predominantly men, and for the particular years included in the sample there were no women. The primary audience for these acceptance addresses are the 1,300 privileged guests at the Nobel banquet, while a secondary audience is the scientific, literary, and general community. Their success stories are told in a public context following the presentation of the award at a ceremonial occasion. Discourse analysis and the constant comparison method are applied to the texts to generate a set of discursive strategies.

In chapter 3, the success stories told by professional and amateur athletes are considered. Newspapers and sporting news magazines are examined for quotations from winning athletes. This sample includes a wide variety of sports and competitors, but the press coverage focuses on sports played predominantly by men. The athletes' stories of success are addressed primarily to fans as consumers of sports news, but a secondary audience includes members of the sports institution (sportswriters, owners, coaches, other players). The stories are mediated, elicited, and edited by sportswriters. Quotations from the athletes are the texts. Discourse analysis and the constant comparison method are used to analyze the acclaiming and disclaiming discourse.

Chapters 4 and 5 explore the success stories of Mary Kay distributors, members of a successful cosmetics company. Two chapters are required to detail the nature of success within this culture and examine the discursive strategies used in telling their success stories. In contrast to the previous analyses, the tellers of these stories are entirely women. Their audience is composed of other women attending Mary Kay functions. The stories arise in an interpersonal setting and are both elicited and spontaneous occurrences. Ethnographic methods are used to detail the nature of success within the group and the acclaiming and disclaiming discourse in the stories of Mary Kay distributors.

Chapter 6 reviews the typology of discursive strategies constructed from the case studies. Similarities and variations in strategies by situation are discussed, and the implications of these findings are considered.

This first chapter has defined success as distinctive and desirable behavior. Success is socially construed, and tellers of success stories are motivated to create self-presentations that shape the meanings of their behaviors for audiences. Research on assertive self-presentation, defensive self-presentation, and self-presentations of success have been reviewed. Tellers of success stories attempt to achieve the multiple goals of securing recognition for a desirable event and appearing modest. Acclaiming discourse includes entitlements and enhancements. By extension, disclaiming discourse includes dissociations and detractions. These self-presentations can be productively viewed as the telling of success stories. Three case studies are selected to develop a typology of discursive strategies for telling the success story.

2   Winning the Prize

Nobel Laureates
Accept the Award

If I have seen farther, it is by standing
on the shoulders of giants.
                    —Isaac Newton,
              on his scientific successes

I think and think for months and years.
Ninety-nine times, the conclusion is
false. The hundredth time I am right.
                    —Albert Einstein,
              recalled on his death

World Championships, Olympic medals, the Cy Young Award, the Louis Jeantet Prize for Medicine, Tonys, Emmys, Oscars, Grammys, Woman of the Year, Man of the Year, the Pulitzer Prize, the Heisman Trophy, and the CLEOs, among others, recognize human accomplishments. It is commonplace to see televised awards or read an article about recent recipients of prizes and awards. Honorees of these formal awards are often in a position to tell their success stories. What do they say? Do their stories acclaim success and disclaim arrogance? Are there similarities in the discursive strategies tellers of success stories use to organize their discourse?

The acceptance addresses of Nobel Award recipients provide an ideal case study of discursive strategies in success stories. Of the myriad awards, the Nobel Prizes are the most prestigious in the entire world (Zuckerman, 1977). They are widely known by the international public and universally recognized in the scientific and literary community. The Nobel Prizes carry a "lofty eminence unmatched by any other honor; to be recognized as a Nobel winner is to be recognized as the best" (Jackson, 1988, p. 220).

Alfred Nobel's (1833–1896) legacy was a controversial handwritten will establishing prizes for "persons who shall have contributed most materially to benefit mankind." Five annual awards were designated for physics, chemistry, medicine/physiology, literature, and peace. In 1968, a sixth award in economic sciences was endowed by the Central Bank of Sweden.

The prizes are financed by the Nobel Foundation, and recipients are selected by committees from the Swedish Royal Academy of Sciences, the Swedish Academy, the Karolinska Institute, and the Norwegian Parliament. The deliberations are secret and the decisions are final. Winners are announced before November 15 and the prizes are awarded on December 10, the anniversary of Nobel's death (Wilhelm, 1983).

This announcement catapults laureates into the public eye. Media attention is particularly intense during the Nobel presentation festivities. A week of press conferences and lectures build toward the presentation ceremony. This ritual includes music, a banquet, the presence of Swedish royalty, presenters' remarks, and the acceptance addresses by awardees. Mulkay's (1984) analysis of presenters' remarks indicates that laureates are "told that they are masters, epoch-makers, standard bearers of intellectual progress and the ultimate source of human welfare" (p. 537). Consistent with the definition of success in the first chapter, laureates are praised for a distinctive behavior: making innovative discoveries or creating literature of great significance. Winners' accomplishments are recognized for improving the human condition through science and the humanities.

Thirteen hundred privileged guests attend the awards ceremony. Secondary audiences include the scientific/literary communities and the general public. Laureates deliver their acceptance addresses to audiences with prior knowledge of their success, and their stories are elicited in the context of a ceremonial occasion. These acceptance addresses tell laureates' success stories. This chapter describes the discourse analytic procedures used to examine the texts of Nobel acceptance addresses and details the strategies organizing the discourse.

METHOD

Nineteen acceptance addresses, reprinted in English in *Les Prix Nobel* (Nobel Foundation, 1967, 1987–1989), were obtained from the winners in 1967 and 1987 through 1989. Each of the Nobel prizes are represented: Chemistry (4), Physics (4), Physiology/Medicine (5), Literature (2), Peace (2), and Economic Science (2). This sample includes winners from Costa Rica (1), Federal Republic of Germany (1), Great Britain (3), Japan (1), Norway (1), Peru (1), Spain (1), Switzerland (1), and the United States (9). The addresses are an average of 18 sentences, varying from 7 to 34 sentences in length.

In the first step of the analysis, statements related to acclaiming and disclaiming success were isolated in the discourse. Strauss describes this process as asking generative questions "essential to making distinctions and comparisons" (1990, p. 17). The texts were examined to find repeated strategies for describing success. Provisional coding of conceptual categories follows and is grounded in the constant comparison method (Glaser & Strauss, 1967; Strauss, 1990). By comparing "indicator to indicator the analyst is forced into confronting similarities, differences, and degrees of consistency of meaning among indicators. This generates an underlying uniformity, which in turn results in a coded category" (Glaser, 1978, p. 62). In this case, sentences reflecting particular acclaiming and disclaiming strategies were compared to assess similarities, differences, and consistency of meaning among sentences coded as the same strategy. As coding proceeded, statements coded as one strategy were contrasted with those coded as other strategies. For example, Müller's comment that "You people in Sweden do these ceremonies with great style and ease" (1987, Physics, p. 39)[1] is coded as complimenting others. It is quite similar to Porter's remark that "we are overawed by the splendor of the occasion tonight" (1967, Chemistry, p. 79); this statement would also be coded in the same category. It became clear as the coding progressed that compliments could be directed to those responsible for the ceremony as well as Alfred Nobel, the people of Sweden, and the selection committee. Thus de Cuéllar's expression that "I should also like to pay homage to the memory of Alfred Nobel, that visionary Scandinavian" (1988, Peace, p. 33) would be coded as a compliment. These statements were contrasted with those coded as other strategies. For instance, Hitchings' remarks that "Each scientific discovery is built upon its predecessors and we give thanks for the dedicated men and women who held tenaciously to their vision and for the legacy of their knowledge" (1988, Physiology/Medicine, p. 38) is coded as sharing credit with others rather than a compliment despite its reference to thanks. Compliments were defined as expressions of thanks directed toward individuals or institutions who were connected to the recognition of the Nobel Prize, while sharing credit emerged as a category to describe the contributions of others to the scientific/literary success with the purpose of distributing the recognition granted by the prize. The constant comparison method promotes the refinement of categories to allow a meaningful picture of the discursive strategies to emerge. Theoretical memos, conceptual sketches written during the process of coding and writing, were used to extend the scope of the explanations and the conceptual density of the analysis (Strauss, 1990).

ANALYSIS

Eleven strategies emerged in the analysis of Nobel acceptance addresses. Table 2.1 provides a complete summary of the discursive strategies generated by this analysis. Consistent with the theoretical framework regarding competing constraints in creating a favorable identity, these strategies were designated as having acclaiming or disclaiming functions in the discourse. Further analysis revealed that issues of responsibility and the importance of a success further organized the strategies. The analysis is divided into sections on acclaiming and disclaiming. The acclaiming section describes entitlements and enhancements. The section on disclaiming describes dissociations and detrac-

TABLE 2.1

A Typology of Strategies for Acclaiming and Disclaiming Discourse in Nobel Acceptance Addresses

---

Acclaiming

Entitlement strategies

1. Tellers recount that they worked hard to earn their success.
2. Tellers report that they persevered in their work.

Enhancement strategies

1. Tellers indicate their success required overcoming obstacles.
2. Tellers demonstrate that their success realized a higher purpose.

Disclaiming

Dissociation strategies

1. Tellers compliment others.
2. Tellers express surprise at their unexpected success or recognition.
3. Tellers share responsibility for their success.
4. Tellers show they are honored or grateful for the recognition.

Detraction strategies

1. Tellers note their success is less noteworthy compared to other accomplishments.
2. Tellers suggest their success is incomplete.
3. Tellers argue their success is limited to a narrow specialty.

---

tions. The particular strategies are compared to the previous literature where it exists.

ACCLAIMING DISCOURSE

Acclaiming discourse explains "a desirable event in a way that maximizes the desirable implications for the actor" (Schlenker, 1980, p. 163). Tellers of success stories reveal that they are to be credited with a significant success. The issue of responsibility for the success is considered first.

Entitlement Strategies

Entitlement strategies claim responsibility for a success. The assumption that labor is required for success is consistent with a cultural belief in the work ethic. Brisbane quips that "the dictionary is the only place where success comes before work" (Reader's Digest, 1975, p. 186). Common proverbs confirm that "diligence is the mistress of success" and "industry is the parent of success" (Mieder, Kingsbury, & Harder, 1992, p. 572). In the two entitlement strategies in Nobel acceptance addresses, tellers (1) recount that they worked hard to earn their success and (2) report that they persevered in their work.

Tellers recount that they worked hard to earn their success. Responsibility is attributed to an individual when an effect is produced intentionally through effort (Martinko, Weiner, & Lord 1995). Tellers of Nobel Prize success stories shape their narratives to reflect the effort they exerted to produce their success. Müller compares the intellectual challenge of his discovery with the difficult physical task of unlocking a door:

> We opened a door in the high-T_c superconductivity field, recognized by the Academy, and you present here share it [our joy] with us as well. (Müller, 1987, Physics, p. 39)

Extraordinary intellectual effort is required to accomplish the task. Recognition is due to the person who leads the way by opening doors for future research. Laureates describe their activities as "effort," "initiatives," "work," and "immense tasks." These activities require hard work and must be produced intentionally.

Tellers report that they persevered in their work. Demonstrating that success is a product of personal effort is accomplished by showing the work required perseverance. The duration of the work displays the devotion of the individual.

> You have given me the Prize I believe for a lifetime of quiet work in physics rather than for any spectacular single contribution. (Berthe, 1967, Physics, pp. 81–82)

> Forty years ago when we began our studies in nucleic acids, we certainly did not anticipate receiving such an award. (Hitchings, 1988, Physiology/Medicine, p. 38)

The recipients call attention to lifetime commitments to their work. Winners toiled long in their laboratories and over the pages of their manuscripts.

The tellers of these success stories describe extraordinary dedication to their work. George Wald, recognized for research on chemical processes of retinal pigments, perseveres in order to understand the molecule and frames his remarks as advice to students.[2]

> I have lived most of my life among molecules. They are good company. I tell my students to try to know molecules, so well that when they have a question involving molecules, they can ask themselves, what would I do if I were that molecule? I tell them, Try to feel like a molecule; and if you work hard, who knows? Some day you may get to feel like a *big* molecule! (Wald, 1967, Physiology/Medicine, p. 38)

Personal causation is more likely to be attributed when there is evidence of exertion and dedication by the individual. Wald spells out a connection between a life dedicated to science and becoming a big molecule upon winning the Nobel Prize. Exertion and dedication entitle him to claim the credit for his successes.

At this juncture, I want to return to the self-presentational literature related to entitlements. Giacalone (1985) and Decker (1987) investigate the effect of taking credit, but they do not examine the nature of the discourse for appropriating that credit. Consistent with Miller, Cooke, Tsang, and Morgan (1992), internal attributions (e.g., effort) were meaningful elements of self-praise. Although Tedeschi and Riess (1981b) predicted that entitlements would appear only when an audience withheld credit, this analysis suggests otherwise. Entitlement strategies are present in the Nobel acceptance addresses even though others have explicitly recognized the success.[3] These findings advance the literature on entitlements by describing the nature of the discourse for accomplishing this purpose and by illustrating the presence of entitlements in situations where responsibility is not disputed.

Enhancement Strategies

Enhancement strategies magnify the worth of an achievement. The more important the recipient's success, the better the story. We are attracted to narratives of great feats rather than to minor accomplishments. Tellers accomplish their self-presentational goals (i.e., creating a favorable identity) by acclaiming significant successes. Enhancement strategies occur when tellers (1) indicate their success required overcoming obstacles and (2) demonstrate that their success realized a higher purpose.

Tellers indicate their success required overcoming obstacles. Success that comes easily, simply, or quickly is not as satisfying or as self-enhancing as a difficult success. The description of a struggle against obstacles is an important element in enhancing a success. In a story, we expect the protagonist to face complications that impede progress before the resolution of the plot line (Campbell, 1956; Frye, 1957). "It is the feeling of exciting effort that exhilarates us, as a grasshopper is exhilarated by jumping. A hard job, full of impediments, is thus more satisfying than an easy one," according to H. L. Mencken (Reader's Digest, 1975, p. 176).

Nobel winners demonstrate they have surmounted obstacles in their journey toward success. Oscar Sánchez received the Nobel Peace Prize for drafting an agreement to reduce hostilities among Nicaragua, Guatemala, Costa Rica, El Salvador, and Honduras. His plan was controversial and required the reluctant cooperation of several parties. In telling his story, Sánchez relates his determination to overcome persistent problems.

> I pay no attention to those doubters and detractors unwilling to believe that a lasting peace can be genuinely embraced by those who march under a different ideological banner or

those who are more accustomed to cannons of war than to councils of peace. (Sánchez, 1987, Peace, p. 35)

Ideological differences and the pessimistic voices of others pose obstacles that fail to deter him from his goal.

In an example from the scientific domain, Sidney Altman describes the difficulties encountered in investigating intricate relationships in nature.

> One of us was working with a strange organism (Tetrahymena thermophila), the other with a familiar organism (Escherichia coli) but with a strange enzyme that somehow needed to carry around an RNA molecule to do its job. Furthermore, neither of our research groups set out in search of RNA catalysis. Thomas Cech and his group initially attributed the activity of their Tetrahymena RNA to a protein contaminant, and they only succumbed to the weight of the accumulated data that argued for the RNA. My group established that Ribonuclease P contained an RNA as well as protein component, and initially there was no reason to suspect that the RNA was responsible for the catalytic activity. Thus, the pathways leading to the discoveries of RNA catalysts were not as direct as one might imagine from reading about the results in textbooks. (Altman, 1989, Chemistry, p. 27)

The research teams struggled with anomalous findings and initially generated inaccurate causal descriptions. Although the path was circuitous, the teller relates that he (and his group) were eventually able to overcome these obstacles to discover that RNA was a catalyst for cell reactions.

Obstacles make success harder to obtain but enhance its value. The more difficult the challenge, the more meritorious their success appears. In recounting the obstacles they managed to overcome, Nobel winners are elevating the importance of their success.

Tellers demonstrate that their success realized a higher purpose. Nobel laureates appear even more praiseworthy by connecting their work to improvements in the human condition.

This strategy asserts that the individual's accomplishments fall within the realm of the culturally construed definition of success described in the first chapter. George Hitchings' prize in Physiology/Medicine was for research on differences between abnormal and normal cells that led to drug treatments designed to act selectively against diseases. He enhances his success by associating his work with applied research.

> We have been further blessed with the privilege of seeing our work become medical therapies to combat diseases like malaria, leukemia, bacterial infections, and gout. (Hitchings, 1988, Physiology/Medicine, p. 38)

His laboratory discoveries improved the human condition by saving lives. The importance of his scientific work in bettering the quality of life secures his acclaim.

Halden Hartline's innovative work demonstrated that the intensity of light affects the speed of the electric impulse in the eye. In his acceptance address, he asserts that such basic research is important in providing a fundamental understanding of the world.

> My second source of satisfaction is that this recognition is for contributions to basic understanding: understanding of primary visual processes . . . If we have succeeded in adding to the basic understanding of our universe and ourselves, we will have made a contribution to the totality of human culture. Scientists care deeply about their place in that culture, and their contribution to it. (Hartline, 1967, Physiology/ Medicine, p. 78)

Scientists' motives, including his own, are characterized as altruistic and Hartline's work is depicted as providing the basic understanding that is a "contribution to the totality of human culture." The value of his work spills over to his personal identity. This strategy enhances the success of the teller by emphasizing the implications of the work in terms of positive values held by the audience.

In comparing these strategies to the prior research on self-enhancements, it is apparent that the literature includes a description of obstacles but neglects the strategy of characterizing their success as realizing a higher purpose. Evidence indicates descriptions of the difficulty of a task magnify the importance of a success (Tedeschi & Riess, 1981b). Nobel winners describe the intellectual and personal obstacles they face and overcome to achieve the behavior being recognized. Mulkay's (1984) analysis of Nobel discourse found evidence that laureates "downgrade specific aspects of their work, without denying the overall significance of their personal achievement" (p. 537). Some of these partial downgrades include descriptions of obstacles. While he does not classify the description of obstacles as self-praise (i.e., acclaiming), I would argue that the outcome of overcoming the obstacles enhances their success. This difference suggests that the strategy may actually accomplish multiple goals simultaneously. The description of the obstacle disclaims, but the narrative regarding the individual's efforts and success in overcoming the obstacle functions as an acclaim.

This analysis of enhancements in Nobel acceptance addresses uncovers a self-enhancement strategy ignored in the literature. Claiming a higher purpose enhances the significance of the success and is consistent with a shared belief (among winners and their audiences) that laureates' contributions improve the human condition.

In summary, this analysis of acclaiming discourse details four discursive strategies. Laureates claim responsibility (i.e., entitlements) by showing they worked to achieve the success and persevered in the work. They emphasize the value of their successes (i.e., enhancements) by describing how they overcame obstacles and contributed to higher goals. The next section considers strategies designed for disclaiming.

DISCLAIMING DISCOURSE

Though laureates want to be recognized, their discourse reflects a competing goal to appear modest for the "worst use that can be made of success is to boast of it" (Mieder, Kingsbury, & Harder, 1992, p. 572). If acclaiming is accomplished by entitlement and enhancement, disclaiming could be expected to have analogous counterparts. These take the form of dissociations that reduce responsibility and detractions that downplay the significance of the success.

Dissociation Strategies

Dissociation strategies reduce the teller's responsibility for the success and are the counterpart of entitlement strategies. When Nobel laureates accept their awards, they exhibit four dissociation strategies. Tellers (1) compliment others, (2) express surprise at their unexpected success or recognition, (3) share responsibility for their success, and (4) show they are honored or grateful for the recognition. These strategies disclaim by redirecting attention, thereby presenting the favorable identity of a modest individual.

Tellers compliment others.   At the presentation ceremony, the presenter of the award begins by praising the Nobel recipient. In the subsequent acceptance address, the laureate returns the compliment and praises others. This avoids appearing pretentious and redresses "the massive self-evaluation brought about by their participation in the Prizegiving ceremonies" (Mulkay, 1984, p. 535). Laureates compliment Alfred Nobel, the prize, the awarding institutions, those responsible for the presentation ceremony, and the governments and people of Sweden and Norway.

> I should also like to pay homage to the memory of Alfred Nobel, that visionary Scandinavian. His commitment to the cause of peace lives on in the Prize which he so generously endowed. (de Cuéllar, 1988, Peace, p. 33)

> Your majesty, these men and all those who worked beside them in exposing the richness of your mineral heritage, have made Sweden great in the realm of chemistry and industry; and in paying tribute to their memory I pay tribute also to the memory of Alfred Nobel, and to the undiminished great-

ness of your country today. Long may it prosper. (Norrish, 1967, Chemistry, p. 80)

My admiration for their wisdom and foresight should go to those persons and institutions who are responsible for the existence of this particular Prize. (Haavelmo, 1989, Economics, p. 30)

The compliments contain strong evaluative language (cf. Mulkay, 1984), describing Nobel as "visionary," Sweden as a country of "undiminished greatness," and the selection committees as possessing "wisdom and foresight." The compliment temporarily locates others in the foreground and the prize recipient modestly in the background.

Tellers express surprise at their unexpected success or recognition. To expect an award is to presume that it is due and is evidence of conceit. To reassure an audience that the award is not expected, their success is explicitly marked as being unanticipated. If the award is unforeseen, the teller of the success story will not be thought to have assumed or coveted the recognition.

Norrish expresses surprise at finding himself a member of an illustrious community for his work on extremely fast chemical reactions.

Stockholm and Uppsala have always beckoned to me as Mecca beckons to the faithful. I little thought to make my pilgrimage [to Sweden] under such auspices as bring me here today. (Norrish, 1967, Chemistry, p. 79)

He tells the audience that he did not foresee that he would find himself a Nobel laureate. He did not expect to win the Prize and be present in Sweden for the presentation ceremony.

In another acceptance address, Hartline contrasts his expectations with the unexpected thrill of winning the Nobel Prize.

One works in one's laboratory—one's chaotic laboratory with students and colleagues, doing what one most wants to do—

then all this happens! It is overwhelming! (Hartline, 1967, Physiology/Medicine, p. 78)

And so, while the daily work is anticipated, the recognition is unpredictable. To say the success is unexpected positions the winner as a modest individual.

Tellers share responsibility for their success with others. The appropriate awarding committee designates those responsible for the work being recognized. Responsibility is not disputed at the presentation ceremony, and so the winner appears quite generous in giving credit to others.[4] Nobel laureates praise others for their professional and personal support. In doing so, the teller is able to "transfer some of the light to them by thanking them in public" (Michel, 1988, Chemistry, p. 38). The following examples illustrate the discourse identifying others as contributors to the laureate's success.

On this very special occasion I wish to extend my sincere gratitude to all my coworkers, technical assistants, and secretaries. Without their interest and devotion, the work recognized by the Nobel assembly would not have been accomplished. (Tonegawa, 1987, Physiology/Medicine, p. 41)

We are also agreed that we owe much to many others, and I would like to mention Professor T.D. Lee, our Columbia colleague, for his guidance and inspiration. I would also like to cite the late Isadore I. Rabi and the department he built at Columbia University in the 1950's and 60's: surely one of the greatest assemblages of physicists ever collected. With six laureates it was ordained that others of us might be infected. We also acknowledge our co-workers on our experiment; all of whom are with us today: Gordon Danby of Brookhaven Laboratory, Jean-Marc Gaillard of CERN/Orsay, Konstantin Goulianos of Rockefeller University, and Nariam Mistry of Cornell. (Lederman, 1988, Physics, p. 36)

I am glad to be able to bring this offering to the memory of my teacher, Selig Hecht, whose widow Celia is here with us tonight; to my wife, who is also my closest co-worker; and

to my co-workers at home, particularly Paul Brown, who for
twenty years has done so much himself, with us all. (Wald,
1967, Physiology/Medicine, p.77)

The first example distributes credit generally to "coworkers,
assistants, and secretaries." The last two instances name specific individuals and provide some detail about the nature of
their contributions.

The previous examples credit other individuals, but responsibility is also granted to social institutions. Sánchez argues
that the Peace Prize honors his country as well as himself.

When you decided to honour me with this prize, you decided
to honour a country of peace, you decided to honour Costa
Rica. (Sánchez, 1987, Peace, p. 34)

Scientists even share the prize with their disciplines, extending
the honor to all those who work within a particular field.

Although we are greatly pleased by being recognized individually, we believe the award also symbolically honors our
entire field of physics, that of high-precision measurements . . .
Many scientists throughout the world are doing beautiful
and accurate measurements. (Ramsey, 1989, Physics, p. 26)

Apart from showing my gratitude with all my heart, I would
like to be permitted to make clear that, if I have dared to
arrive where I am now, it is only because I understand that the
Prize is not just being awarded to me, but also to my contem-
poraries who write in the glorious language which is our tool:
Spanish. (Cela, 1989, Literature, pp. 29–30)

The award is shared explicitly with the larger community of
physicists who do "beautiful and accurate measurements" and
writers who "write in the glorious language" of Spanish. The
laureate appears modest by exhibiting a willingness to appor-
tion the honor among others.

Tellers show they are honored or grateful for the recognition.
The Nobel Prize secures considerable recognition for the

recipient. Recipients are expected to accept the recognition but understand that it is granted at the discretion of the Nobel Foundation. Individuals cannot give themselves awards but depend upon others to recognize their achievements. Thus, the recipient is obligated to be appreciative. Expressing honor or gratitude demonstrates that the recipient is properly thankful for the recognition provided by the selection committee and the audience.

Hartmut Michel, the winner in Chemistry in 1988, offers sincere thanks to the Royal Swedish Academy for endorsing his success.

> In this light, also on behalf of Hans Deisenhofer and Robert Huber, I would like to sincerely thank the Royal Swedish Academy of Science for shining light on us by this ultimate recognition. (Michel, 1988, Chemistry, p. 16)

Receiving the award in Physiology/Medicine, Halden Hartline begins his acceptance presentation by describing his personal appreciation and his inability to convey his reaction.

> I wish I could adequately express my feelings of pleasure and deep gratitude for this great honor that has come to me. But of course this is impossible—one cannot convey one's personal feelings on such an occasion as this. (Hartline, Physiology/Medicine, 1967, pp. 77–78)

In expressing gratitude, the teller of the success story thanks others for the tremendous recognition and discharges the implied obligation. Gratitude is marked as "sincere" and the honor is "great." The laureate presents himself as unassuming and unpretentious in expecting the success but appreciative when it is granted.

A comparison to the prior research is now in order. The strategy of complimenting others is recognized as a self-enhancement technique (Aronson & Linder, 1965; Kipnis & Vanderveer, 1971; Mette, 1971). Pomerantz's (1978) analysis of competing constraints and Mulkay's (1984) application to Nobel discourse are suggestive of the function compliments play in disclaiming. A redirected compliment avoids self-praise. Nobel winners avoid excessive self-praise by complimenting others.

The strategy of expressing surprise at an unexpected success or recognition is mentioned briefly by Miller, Cooke, Tsang, and Morgan (1992). In one of four situations tested, they discovered that surprise, rather than bragging, was associated with a positive description, suggesting it could function as disclaiming discourse.

The third strategy shares responsibility for the success. Previous research suggests that audiences evaluate individuals positively who share credit (Decker, 1987, 1990) and that sharing credit is associated with positive self-descriptions and not bragging (Miller, Cooke, Tsang, & Miller, 1992). Mulkay (1984) confirms these reassignments of praise as a dominant form of Nobel discourse. Allocating credit to others disclaims partial responsibility.

Nobel laureates indicate that they are honored or grateful for the award in a fourth dissociation strategy. In the context of receiving a formal award, the awarding institution and the audience expect appreciation for the recognition. Mulkay (1984) includes appreciations as compliments. They may both disclaim, but they are conceptually distinct forms. Compliments praise others for desirable characteristics and attributes. Expressions of gratitude and honor for a recognition articulate the inner state of the recipient upon receiving the award.

Detraction Strategies

Detraction strategies are the counterpart of enhancements and reduce the significance of a success. In these strategies, tellers: (1) note their success is less noteworthy compared to other accomplishments, (2) suggest their success is incomplete, and (3) argue their success is limited to a narrow specialty. Although their achievements remain impressive, the laureate's attempts to minimize their accomplishments create a modest self-presentation.

Tellers note their success is less noteworthy compared to other accomplishments. This form of modesty compares a laureate's success with the accomplishments of other individuals, particularly prior recipients of the prize and respected scientists/authors in the relevant disciplines.

> I feel quite humble comparing myself with many of my predecessors who have made great and fundamental discoveries. (Berthe, 1967, Physics, p. 81)

> The Swedish Academy is honouring me by inscribing my name in the margins of the roll of illustrious personages of contemporary world literature. It is an honour which is out of all proportion to my skill and ability. (Cela, 1989, Literature, p. 29)

In these instances, strong and positive evaluative language is used to characterize the comparison group (e.g., "great," "illustrious") and the laureate devalues his own personal skills and abilities in the comparison. The detraction strategy creates a modest impression even though the audience is well aware that the social comparison is being made with those already recognized as extraordinary individuals.

Tellers suggest their success is incomplete. This strategy is based on a comparison of past or present accomplishments with future goals. The success is incomplete because salient goals are unrealized. Harold Varmus was honored for discovering that cancer-causing genes associated with a virus were derived from altered cellular genes. This work was hailed as an important advance in cancer research, but he characterizes the fight as ongoing.

> We recognize that, unlike Beowulf at the hall of Hrothgar, we have not slain our enemy, the cancer cell, or figuratively torn the limbs from his body. In our adventures, we have only seen our monster more clearly and described his scales and fangs in new ways—ways that reveal a cancer cell to be, like Grendel, a distorted version of our normal selves. May

this new vision and the spirit of tonight's festivities inspire
our band of biological warriors to inflict much greater wounds
tomorrow. (Varmus, 1989, Physiology/Medicine, p. 28)

In the battle against cancer, Varmus' contribution is down-
graded from the status of winning a complete victory to that
of winning one skirmish in an ongoing war.

For Camilio José Cela, the goal of literature is "to give
justice its rightful place by rendering to everyone what is his,
and by understanding and upholding good laws" (p. 30). Yet,
the work of writers, including Cela, is unfinished.

I am aware that we have not reached the goal that we are
aiming at, and that there are still many steps to be taken in
serenity and good sense, with constancy, no doubt, but also
with luck. I propose that we never wander off this salubrious
road. (Cela, 1989, Literature, p. 30)

The contribution of any single individual seems less conse-
quential in comparison to such lofty goals.

Tellers argue their success is limited to a narrow specialty. An
institutional norm of humility is prevalent in science such that
"scientists insist upon their personal limitations and the limitations of knowledge" (Merton, 1957a, p. 646). The winners
of the Nobel Prize gain immediate and far-reaching expertise
power. Laureates are quick to enact the norm of humility to
restrict the scope of their knowledge. Tongue in cheek, they
joke about the unrealistic expectations concerning their new
found wisdom.

Seven weeks have gone by since it became known that I had
won this Prize. During that time I have been asked to solve
the economic problems of the United States, Norway, Sweden, the Federal Republic of Germany, Israel, Spain, Portu-
gal, Argentina, Brazil, Mexico, the Philippines, China, Japan,
and Korea. It goes without saying that I know the answers
to all those questions, but it would be unfair to tell you so
soon. (Solow, 1987, Economics, pp. 41–42)

> My colleagues Melvin Schwartz and Jack Steinberger join me
> to express our feelings of pleasure and gratitude for the
> decision to award us the 1988 Nobel Prize for Physics, thus
> making us experts on the Brazilian debt, women's fashions
> and social security. (Lederman, 1988, Physics, p. 36)

The winners' ironic exaggerations make the point that their
success has restricted boundaries, and the recognition of the
Nobel Prize has not expanded their expertise. This detraction
strategy reveals the humility of the recipient by limiting the
scope of the accomplishment to a narrow specialty.

These three detraction strategies minimize the importance
of the success. Detraction strategies have not been previously
examined in the literature. This analysis of Nobel acceptance
addresses provides a significant advance in our understanding
of discourse organized to minimize the significance of a success.

In summary, seven disclaiming strategies have been described.
Nobel Prize winners reduce their responsibility (i.e., dissociations) by complimenting others, expressing surprise at their
success or recognition, sharing responsibility for their success,
and showing they are honored by or grateful for the recognition. They downplay the significance of their success (i.e.,
detractions) by comparing their success to other accomplishments, indicating their success is incomplete, and showing that
their success is limited to a narrow specialty.

DISCUSSION

The prominence of the Nobel Prize secures international attention and elevates the salience of self-presentational goals.[5] This
chapter describes the discursive strategies for acclaiming and
disclaiming in Nobel acceptance addresses.

Acclaiming secures recognition through entitlements and
enhancements. Entitlements shape an audience's attributions of
responsibility by describing internal causes for the success. This
discourse makes use of literal and metaphorical language to
characterize the laureate's behavior as work and posit the in-

ternal disposition of perseverance as a causal explanation for the success. Discursive strategies turned toward enhancement describe the significance of the success through reliance on cultural values. The value of improving the human condition and a conviction that obstacles can be overcome are commonly accepted beliefs.

Disclaiming discourse attends to the modesty constraint on success stories through dissociations and detractions. Dissociations reduce responsibility for the success. Laureates redirect self-praise by complimenting others and sharing responsibility for the success. In addition, the strategies of expressing surprise and displaying gratitude for the prize highlight the relationship between granter and recipient. While the granter bestows the honor, recipients are expected to appropriately acknowledge their indebtedness. By expressing surprise and gratitude, the laureate appears unassuming and accepts the granter's right to bestow the honor. Detraction strategies minimize the importance of the success by erecting a comparison for the audience. Tellers claim their success is less noteworthy compared to others' accomplishments, unrealized goals, and the possible breadth of knowledge. These comparisons discursively reframe the success and position the laureate as humble in his estimation of its overall importance.

Telling the success story is a precarious and fascinating balancing act because competing constraints define the situation. The teller wants to be recognized as successful. Success is a predominant cultural value and motivator, and tellers require the cooperation of others in bestowing and recognizing their accomplishments. Acclaiming strategies can create a desired identity and are the most direct route to securing recognition. But the teller must avoid excessive self-praise, and violating this expectation risks a negative impression. Disclaiming strategies are the most direct route to a modest and positively evaluated identity. But minimizing responsibility and the importance of the success risks the recognition desired and may be seen as disagreeing with the decision of the granter of the award. How are competing constraints enacted in discourse? How do Nobel laureates weight the scales in their balancing act?

Mulkay (1984) argues that self-praise (i.e., acclaiming) is rare in Nobel discourse because the presentation ceremony, with the laudatory comments of the presenter, tip the scales toward compliment returns, partial downgrades, and reassignments of praise (i.e., disclaiming). My analysis confirms that awardees emphasize disclaiming in Nobel acceptance addresses. Nobel winners exhibit more developed strategic choices and devote more time to disclaiming than to acclaiming.

Norman Ramsey's acceptance address is reprinted with statement numbers to illustrate the relative emphasis on disclaiming in a Nobel acceptance address:

> On behalf of Wolfgang Paul, Hans Dehmelt and myself, I wish to express our deepest thanks for the honors granted to us today. [1] For me, it is a double pleasure to share this award with two such distinguished fellow physicists. [2]
>
> The three of us have neither collaborated nor competed on any experiment, but we have shared the common goals of seeking new methods for precise measurements and applying these methods to obtain fundamental properties of molecules, atoms, and elementary particles. [3]
>
> Although we are greatly pleased by being recognized individually, we believe the award also symbolically honors our entire field of physics, that of high-precision measurements. [4] The award reminds the world that Physics is an experimental science and can still be successfully pursued in a university laboratory. [5] Many scientists throughout the world are doing beautiful and accurate measurements. [6] We believe that research of this nature will continue to make major contributions to the understanding of the fundamental laws of our universe. [7] (Ramsey, 1989, Physics, pp. 26–27)

Ramsey disclaims in expressing gratitude for the award (1) and complimenting the two physicists with whom he shares the award (2). In statement four, he expresses gratitude for the recognition again and shares credit with the entire field of physics. He compliments the work of other scientists involved in precision measurement (6) and suggests that the work is incomplete (7). Acclaiming is present in the description of new methods for discovering fundamental properties (3) and the assertion that such work improves the human condition through understanding the laws of nature (7). Five of the seven strategies disclaim the success. Taken as a whole, the teller of this particular success story redirects attention away from himself and onto the granter of the award, corecipients, other scientists, and the discipline of physics but is also able to assert the importance of his work.

In important ways, my analysis departs from Mulkay's (1984) treatment of Nobel discourse as a ceremonial response to a compliment. The explanatory framework for his analysis rests on preference for agreement, yet many of the disclaiming strategies I found are not explained by this concept. Mulkay's focus on the Nobel discourse as a response to the ultimate compliment causes him to attend to discourse that avoids disagreement and self-praise. The goal of securing recognition, distinct from simply avoiding disagreement, is not included.

This case study of Nobel acceptance addresses as success stories confirms the use of particular strategies from the literature on self-presentation and unearths several unique strategies. Nobel laureates were chosen because the prize carries tremendous eminence and the presentation ceremony is clearly an occasion for telling a success story. This chapter reveals how they organize their discourse to respond to competing constraints.

Success stories are elicited at award ceremonies. As I was revising this chapter, I caught excerpts from the Golden Globe awards. In 1996, Mel Gibson won the best director award for *Braveheart* and said, "I didn't expect to get this," illustrating surprise. The producer of *Babe* shared credit in remarking, "A lot of people helped bring this little pig to life." A few weeks later I attended a dinner for recipients of teaching awards on campus. The winners expressed their surprise at being singled out for this honor and thanked their teachers and colleagues. I was fascinated by the similarity of the talk of actors, teachers, and Nobel laureates when they found themselves in a situation where they won an award and were expected to just "say a few words."

3

The Thrill of Victory
Athletes Tell Their Success Stories

It's hard not to play golf that's up to Jack Nicklaus standards when you are Jack Nicklaus.

—Jack Nicklaus,
on winning his seventieth
PGA Tournament

A team championship doesn't happen because three people score 10s, it happens because all the guys score well. In my opinion, everyone deserves 10s, we're all 10s on the team.

—Mitch Gaynor,
1984 Olympic gold medalist

Sports pervade our society. Their widespread influence is exhibited in "news coverage, financial expenditures, number of participants and spectators, movies, books, themes in comic strips, hours consumed, sales of sports equipment, and time sampling of conversations" (Snyder & Spreitzer, 1978, p. 1). Ninety-six percent of the American population frequently plays, watches, or reads articles about sports (Vecsey, 1983). Sports permeate popular culture.

Winning is highly valued. Successful athletes are held in high esteem by sports fans. The emphasis on competitiveness and individual achievement provides fertile ground for the analysis of success stories. Athletes' descriptions of their successes are strategic accomplishments. This chapter is organized by a consideration of the relevant literature, the nature of success in sports, a description of method, and the analysis of statements made by athletes in articles covering sports events.

PREVIOUS LITERATURE

The relevant literature considers the embodiment of cultural values in sports and media coverage and the attributional biases in athletes' characterizations of their successes. Theorists argue that sports enjoy tremendous regard because they closely reflect dominant values of achievement and success present in the culture (Williams, 1970). Character building, discipline, competition, physical fitness, mental fitness, religiosity, and nationalism are the principles of the American sports creed (Edwards, 1973). Athletes are directed to work hard in order to succeed. They are promised that there will be equal opportunity to excel and that hard work will be rewarded (Nixon, 1984). These values are instantiated in locker room slogans like:

> The harder I work, the luckier I get.
> You're as good as you want to be.
> Who passed the ball to you when you scored?
> Winning beats anything that comes in second. (Snyder, 1972)

The values conveyed to Little League players by coaches include sportsmanship, teamwork, and winning/losing (Fine, 1978). Lipsky (1978) contends that "the sports aesthetic can be seen as facilitating the internalization of the 'proper' attitudes toward mobility, success, and competition. In this way, sports is the symbolic expression of the values of the larger political and social milieu" (p. 351). Stories about success are expected to reference these cultural values.

Media coverage of sporting events reaffirms cultural values. Trujillo and Ekdom's (1985) analysis of the coverage of the 1984 Chicago Cubs reveals six sets of oppositional cultural values in sporting news stories: winning and losing, tradition and change, teamwork and individualism, work and play, youth and experience, and logic and luck. In a similar study of sportswriters' descriptions of the Dallas Cowboys, Vande Berg and Trujillo (1989) show that stories emphasize process (e.g., "be the best you can be") when the team is losing and product (e.g., "win the game") when the team is winning. Announcers for televised football used commentary that heightened conflict and addressed the themes of competence, gamesmanship, comparisons, and the "old college try" (Bryant, Comisky, & Zillmann, 1977).[1]

In the sports psychology literature, athletes' attributions for success (and failure) have been examined. Several studies (Croxton & Klonsky, 1982; Iso-Ahola, 1975; Riordan, Thomas, & James, 1985; Taylor & Doria, 1981; Zientek & Breakwell, 1991) document a self-serving bias (i.e., internal attributions for wins and external attributions for losses) among athletes. Weiner's (1979) attributional model predicts that individuals will attribute their successes to internal, stable, and controllable causes. While gymnasts' explanations of successful performances confirmed Weiner's predictions, in a separate study Mark, Mutrie, Brooks, and Harris (1984) did not find a difference in the locus of causality, although winners were more likely to make stable and controllable attributions. Stable attributions are more likely after expected outcomes (Lau & Russell, 1980). This research examines the maintenance of self-esteem through attributional biases rather than the self-presentational function of particular attributions directed to audiences (Leary, 1992). As athletes tell their success stories to audiences, it is "the process by which individuals attempt to control the impressions others form of them" (Leary & Kowalski, 1990, p. 34; Leary, 1992) that is the focus of attention.

Our culture's preoccupation with success is played out in sporting events and rendered newsworthy by media. Athletes and sportswriters collaborate in telling a good story for fans. Such a narrative is also a recognizable story because it makes reference to commonly accepted cultural values. The attributional literature indicates the importance of claiming responsibility to improve self-esteem but does not consider the self-presentational goals that can be achieved by these attributions. This analysis will examine the mediated statements of successful athletes as opportunities to shape fans' impressions of their performance.

THE NATURE OF SUCCESS IN SPORTS

Within the sports institution, successes are defined as making a significant play, winning a game, receiving an award for athletic performance, breaking a record, and winning a championship or medal. These successes are depicted as "objective" measures of outcomes. Except for the significant play, successes are "factified." The earned run average of a baseball player, the number of assists for a basketball player, the type of Olympic medal won, the final score in a game are constructed as irrefutable evidence of a success. Cheska argues that this ritualistic feature is attractive to sports fans for "the simplicity of the game stands in orderly contrast to the complicated, confused, chaotic world of power transactions. In the real world of social transactions it is difficult to know if one has won or lost" (Cheska, 1979, p. 57). On the other hand, in the world of sports, everyone knows the winner.

However, not all sports successes are equal. The relative importance of a sports success is a matter of negotiated meaning about the value of performances. Generally plays are the smallest unit within games and least valued, while championships involve a series of games and are more valued. The "scarcity of the prize" and the distinctiveness of the performance determine its relative value (Figler & Whitaker, 1991).

An athlete earns prestige and economic rewards from success. Sports figures acquire fame and are admired by fans. The culture rewards top players with economic symbols of success. For instance, Michael Jordan earned $13 million from sports endorsements within a year (Agins, 1992). There is a great deal at stake when an athlete tells a success story.

Athletes' stories are elicited and mediated. If an athlete performs well, that person is likely to be interviewed. And if the athlete's statement is judged "newsworthy," it appears in an article read by fans. But direct statements from athletes compete for space with sportswriters' descriptions of plays, interpretations of the strengths and weaknesses of athletes and teams, and predictions about future performances. Athletes' direct statements are edited. Athletes competing in major sports (football, basketball, baseball, Olympics) and acknowledged stars of the game (e.g., Michael Jordan, Nolan Ryan, Joe Montana) get many opportunities to tell their stories to sportswriters, who then retell them to fans. Many daily newspapers allocate more space to sports than any other topic (Klein, 1979), and research reports that 30 percent of readers bought newspapers primarily to read the sports section (Edwards, 1973). *Sport* and *Sports Illustrated* have 930,000 and 3.1 million subscribers respectively (Bowker, 1995). Fans are reading about sporting events, including the stories reported about athletes' successes.

METHOD

Articles about sporting events from the wire services in local newspapers and those appearing in *Sports Illustrated*, *The Sporting News*, *Sport*, *The Boston Sunday Globe*, *The Chicago Tribune*, *USA Today*, and the *New York Times* were reviewed for direct statements from winning athletes. The statements of coaches and owners were excluded. Also, only self-praise was analyzed, so statements by athletes who praised their teammates were also excluded. Statements were collected during a nine-month period in 1990 and a six-month period in 1992. This included coverage of every major professional and amateur sport and the 1992 Summer and Winter Olympic competitions. The Olympics were included because they represent the "top rung of the organized sports hierarchy in the United States" (Nixon, 1984, p. 25) in many sports for which there is no professional competition. A total of 377 statements from 255 athletes were identified.

The discourse was initially reviewed through repeated readings and the notation of recurring message strategies with attention directed toward discourse that shaped attributions about successful performances. In a preliminary analysis, statements that appeared to use similar strategies were categorized together. Statements were placed in more than one category if they exhibited multiple discourse strategies. Through the use of the constant comparative method, described in some detail in chapter 2, each statement was compared to other statements. For example, Joe Magrane, a Cardinals pitcher, commented after a win against the Mets: "I've been pretty fortunate against this club. But Omar [Olivares] and Lee [Smith] really got the big outs" ("Magrane," 1990, p. 13B). This statement was initially coded as sharing the credit with others because Magrane identified the relief pitchers as contributing significantly to the win. This statement was compared with others that had been previously coded as sharing credit to assess the fit with this category. During this process, a decision is made to retain the original coding, recode the statement, code the statement in multiple categories, or revise the category description. In this case, the statement was coded in multiple categories because Magrane also makes reference to his good fortune in playing against the Mets; this is similar to other statements coded as claiming external or uncontrollable causes for a success. This constant comparative method led to amendments of the initial categorizations and continuous revisions of the descriptions of discursive strategies as categories. Counterexamples were sought to refine the analysis and reduce the confirmationist bias (Jacobs, 1988). Theoretical memos were written to refine the theoretical framework and were used to "yield conceptually dense theory" (Strauss, 1990, p. 17). The statements were entered, identified by strategy or strategies, and sorted by ETHNOGRAPH, a computer program designed to systematically retrieve segments of text by codes assigned by the analyst. Further refinements were made in the analysis. The presentation of the analysis is dependent upon examples to display the "rich, concrete reality" from which the description evolved.

ANALYSIS

A total of 15 strategies emerged in the analysis of athletes' self-presentations. Table 3.1 provides a complete summary of the discursive strategies generated by this analysis. The analysis is

TABLE 3.1

A Typology of Strategies for Acclaiming and Disclaiming Discourse in Athletes' Statements

Acclaiming

Entitlement strategies

1. Tellers report that they persevered in their work.

2. Tellers describe their self-motivation.

Enhancement strategies

1. Tellers indicate their success required overcoming obstacles.

2. Tellers associate their success with the achievements of great individuals in their field.

3. Tellers describe their success as the apex of their ability.

4. Tellers indicate their success may not be repeatable.

5. Tellers show their success was a turning point.

6. Tellers demonstrate that their success is superior to others.

7. Tellers describe their success as fulfilling a dream.

Disclaiming

Dissociation strategies

1. Tellers attribute their success to external or uncontrollable causes.

2. Tellers express surprise at their unexpected success or recognition.

3. Tellers share responsibility for their success.

Detraction strategies

1. Tellers note their success is less noteworthy compared to other accomplishments.

2. Tellers suggest their success is incomplete.

3. Tellers indicate their success is flawed.

---

divided into sections on acclaiming as it is accomplished through entitlement and enhancement strategies, and disclaiming as it is enacted through dissociations and detractions. Comparisons are made to the discursive strategies of Nobel winners as described in chapter 2.

ACCLAIMING DISCOURSE

While there are intrinsic rewards in simply playing the game, the sports institution values product more than process and promises athletes that success on the playing field will translate to prestige and prosperity. Like others, athletes enact behaviors that maximize rewards. Initially, this means playing well enough to make an extraordinary play, win a game, receive an award, break a record, or win a championship/medal, for these are the yardsticks for measuring success. But even "objectified" sports successes are subject to interpretation. "Facts" can be construed and negotiated, leading individuals to "attempt to control the attributions others make about them in order to maximize their own reward/cost ratios" (Schlenker, 1980, p. 25). Athletes may be led to expect recognition, but to secure it they acclaim through entitlement and enhancement strategies.

Entitlement Strategies

Recognition is reserved for individuals who are responsible for a success (D'Arcy, 1963). Athletes attempt to shape sports fans' attributions through self-descriptions that attribute the success to an internal and controllable cause. In asserting responsibility for a success, tellers (1) report that they persevered in their work and (2) describe their self-motivation.

Tellers report that they persevered in their work. Gwen Torrence won an Olympic gold medal in the 200-meter dash. Her self-presentation tells what *she* did to be successful:

> I had to work five long, tough years, and it finally came. ("U.S. Struts Golden Stuff," 1992, p. 1B)

The work involved a substantial amount of time, and it did not come easily. Achievement is attributed to the controllable and internal actions taken by the athlete over an extensive period of time. Athletes remind audiences that the few moments of an actual athletic performance are made possible through years of training.

Mark Lenzi won the three-meter springboard diving competition at the 1992 Summer Olympics. He describes how the work he and his coach did on a particular dive was important to his success.

> I was thinking Kimball puts me in the belts every morning for so long that this better really pay off. And it did. We worked really hard on my twisters. ("Former Wrestler Dives," 1992, p. 3B)

Lenzi asserts a causal relationship between working hard and winning. And although credit for the success is shared with the coach, the audience understands that it is the athlete who performed the lengthy physical exertions in the belts.

This strategy for acclaiming makes reference to one of the basic principles of sports competition: hard work pays dividends. The athlete who uses this self-presentation reconfirms cultural values that assert that success is the product of hard work and that athletes who make an extraordinary effort should receive a commensurate reward.

Hard work is an internal and controllable attribution. An individual must consciously decide to engage in hard work; thus it is under the actor's control. Others can cajole or offer advice, but it is the athlete who must actually engage in the physical and mental effort. In depicting an internal cause for the success, an athlete is claiming responsibility (Leith, 1989; Weiner, 1986; Zientek & Breakwell, 1991).

Tellers describe their self-motivation. Motivation is an inner drive or intention that causes a person to act in ways consistent with goals. Success is the product of motivation and attributable to the athlete. It is a common belief in the sports culture that "individuals can directly and indirectly influence the performance and behavior by directing their thoughts and actions through conscious efforts" (Harris & Harris, 1984, p. 118). Athletes tell fans that they did this by self-motivating talk during competitions. Hale Irwin reports on his self-talk:

> I just kept pecking away . . . told myself to keep going, keep
> going. ("Irwin Goes Overtime," 1990, p. 11B)

As he plays each hole on the sprawling course, he keeps himself motivated and confident to succeed.

The motivation to win accounts for extraordinary plays by
an athlete. In 1990, the Red Sox triumphed three to one over
the White Sox for the American League title. Tom Brunansky
caught a ball hit by Ozzie Guillen, depicting his attempts to do
so as the consummate effort.

> I knew I was going into the wall for it. Either I was going
> to get it, or I'd kill myself. ("Red Sox Defeat Ghosts," 1990,
> p. 17)

The drive to win, to make that important catch, causes athletes
to "go the distance." Attributing success to the motivation to
excel is internal and controllable, so the athlete is presented as
the agent responsible for the success.

Athletes are held accountable for their behaviors in a competition (Edwards, 1973) and their discursive strategies can
influence attributions regarding success. Just as Nobel laureates articulated their intellectual perseverance, athletes describe
the physical effort required to succeed. Athletes also describe
their motivation to succeed. These entitlement strategies elaborate the internal dispositions that make it possible for an athlete to win (Miller, Cooke, Tsang, & Morgan, 1992).

Enhancement Strategies

Important successes enhance the reputation of an athlete. Rewards are commensurate with the level of success. While there
is shared meaning within the sports institution about the hierarchy of types of sports successes, athletes can negotiate the
importance of a particular accomplishment. Athletes displayed
seven enhancement strategies for embellishing their successes.
Tellers indicate that their personal success (1) required overcoming obstacles, (2) is associated with the achievements of

great individuals in their field, (3) represents the apex of their ability, (4) may not be repeatable, (5) was a turning point, (6) was superior to others, and (7) fulfilled a dream.

Tellers indicate their success required overcoming obstacles. The St. Louis Cardinals beat the New York Mets seven to five in the 1990 season. Rex Hudler describes the Mets as tough competition.

> We could have a 10-run lead in the late innings, and it wouldn't mean much against the Mets. They're the best team in the league by far, right now. ("Cards Sidestep Mets' Comeback," 1990, p. 13B)

By beating the best team, the reputation of the winning team and its players is enhanced. Despite the very real obstacles of the opposition's skill and talent, the athlete is able to succeed.

Physical obstacles can pose a formidable barrier for athletes. Gail Devers contracted Grave's disease and could not walk in 1991. The next year she overcame her disease and won a gold medal in the 100-meter dash. She describes this obstacle and the importance of the victory.

> I didn't think I'd ever run again. ("Sprinter Completes Comeback," 1992, p. 1B)

> It just feels great. This was a long time coming. It means my Grave's disease is over. I'm back where I wanted to be, so it feels great. ("Devers Conquers All," 1992, p. 25)

While Devers could not prevent the disease, she could decide how to respond to it. She describes the severity of the disease to a runner and her self-presentation makes it clear that she has acted in ways that allowed her to conquer the disease.

An obstacle stands in the way of victory and an athlete who describes overcoming adversity to win magnifies the importance of the success. Nixon (1984) confirms that a common theme in sports stories is "that seemingly insurmountable obstacles to success are overcome by relentless dedication and hard work" (p. 10).

Tellers associate their success with the achievements of great individuals in their field. Larry Laoretti won the 1992 U.S. Senior Open by four strokes. It was his first tournament win on the Senior Tour, and he enhances the importance of the success by reminding fans that Jack Nicklaus, the "Golden Bear" of golf fame, won the same tournament.

> I got my name next to Nicklaus and that's what I like to see. ("Smoking the Field," 1992, p. 10B)

Laoretti is in good company. His own success appears that much better for having been associated with a well-known sports figure.

In capturing the American League baseball record for most career steals during the 1990 season, Rickey Henderson broke Ty Cobb's record. He enhances the success by suggesting that it is surpassed only by Lou Brock's all-time record.

> I realized when I slid into third and I didn't see a tag that it was all over for being number one in the American League. Lou Brock is number one all-time, but this fits right up there. ("Henderson Shifts," 1990, p. 11B)

By association, Henderson's accomplishment is amplified. Basking in reflected glory (Cialdini, 1989; Cialdini, Borden, Thorne, Walker, Freeman, & Sloan, 1976), the athlete's success is more significant for being related to a sports figure that fans recognize as a sports great.

Tellers describe their success as the apex of their ability. Gibby Gilbert won the 1992 Kroger Senior Golf Classic by shooting seven under par and describes the success as a career high:

> This is by far the best I've played in my life. ("Gilbert Overtakes Snead," 1992, p. 3B)

The success is significant because it is unparalleled in Gibby Gilbert's long experience in playing golf. This comparison involves a judgment of an athlete's present prowess compared to past performances.

Pete Sampras reflects that his easy win in four sets over John McEnroe in the semifinals of the U.S. Open represents his best play.

> Today was the best I could possibly play. I think this was the best match I've played all two weeks and all year. ("Sampras Makes," 1990, p. 9)

This match is compared to his recent matches during the U.S. Open tournament and his matches during the season to substantiate his judgment of its excellence.

Athletes describe a particular play or game as the highest point they have achieved in the sport. It makes the success significant because it is favorably distinguished from past successes, being celebrated as distinctive for the individual involved.

Tellers indicate their success may not be repeatable. An indisputable fact in sports is that physical control over the body declines over time. The career of a professional athlete or Olympic contestant is limited. This fact explains sports stories about Mary Ellen Clark as the oldest diver on the Olympic Team or the "Old Man" of tennis, Jimmy Connors, when it appears that he may win again. Their successes are particularly important because they may represent the last opportunity for that athlete to succeed.

At 33, Martina Navratilova had already won four U.S. Open singles titles. She was the "Grand Dame" of tennis and proceeded to win a match against Britain's Clare Wood in 1990. She emphasizes the importance of her success by commenting on her age.

> When you are 17 or 18, you figure you have 20 more U.S. Opens to go. I don't have that many to go. Everyone could

> be my last one, so it is precious. ("Navratilova Moves On,"
> 1990, p. 15B)

The success is enhanced by directing the attention of others to
the fact that it may not occur again.

Because the Olympics occur every four years, athletes often
have a single chance to excel in this prestigious competition. The
opportunity to even compete may not be repeatable because it
is difficult to sustain peak performance until the next Olympics
occur. Ronny Weller won a gold medal in weight lifting at the
1992 Olympics, lifting 953¼ pounds in his best snatch and
clean and jerk lifts. He directs attention to the importance of the
success as it represents a last chance for him to medal.

> I have been waiting for this moment all my life. It was a case
> of now or never. ("German Lifter Makes Comeback," 1992,
> p. 7)

Time was running out; it was "now or never." Weller may not
be able to repeat an appearance at the Olympics and has
grabbed this chance to succeed. Because success is fleeting with
age, a last (or nearly so) occurrence ought to be more valued.
The success is more difficult to achieve and consequently more
distinctive.

Tellers show their success was a turning point.   A turning
point is an athletic achievement that occurs at a crucial point
in a game, series, or championship. It is responsible for changing the energy and outcome of a competition. It is the point at
which victory becomes possible.

During the 1990 football season, Mike Bell recovered the
football for the Kansas City Chiefs as the Raiders were about
to tie the game. There were 12 minutes to play and Los An-
geles fumbled at the Chiefs' 27 yard line. Mike Bell tells fans
that he believes his actions could have been critical.

> When I jumped on the ball, everyone was just trying to tear
> it loose. I was just hanging on for dear life. It could have

been the turning point because it stopped their drive down deep in our territory. ("KC Downs Raiders," 1990, p. 11B)

In nine subsequent plays, the Chiefs gained 93 yards and won 27 to 17. Bell retrospectively identifies his own action as potentially instrumental to the win. He also depicts his own actions as difficult, battling against "everyone" and "hanging on for dear life." An extraordinary play is made more so by having occurred at a pivotal position in the game.

Excitement ran high in game two of the 1990 NBA Championship Series. Clyde Drexler sunk two free throws with two seconds remaining. This gave the Portland Trail Blazers a win after having lost game one to the Detroit Pistons. Drexler characterizes the game as key to the series.

> This was the most exciting game I've ever played in at the most exciting time. This game was really sweet for us. It gave us the homecourt advantage back. Now, we think the series is in our favor. ("Drexler Keeps His Promise," 1990, p. 16B)

He projects that the win will be the key to the outcome of the series, emphasizing the importance of his actions. This win is presented as more important than other games because it occurs in the championship series, follows a loss, retrieves the homecourt advantage, and is accomplished through Drexler's extraordinary play.

Athletes who can make the big plays are especially valued because their contributions are more significant to the outcome of a competition. A significant play becomes more than the display of athleticism when it occurs at a critical moment. A win is more than a victory when it influences the outcome (potential or actual) of a championship. A sports success is elevated in importance when an athlete connects it to a higher level of success (e.g., plays to wins, game wins to championships). The strategy of identifying a success as a turning point allows athletes to demonstrate to sports fans that their success is momentous.

Tellers demonstrate that their success is superior to others. A performance can be remarkable because it greatly surpasses the competition. Jorg Hoffmann, competing in the Olympics, compares himself to other swimmers.

> I always ask myself where others find the courage to swim against me. (Murphy, 1992, p. 66)

The boast downgrades competitors and enhances the abilities of the acclaiming athlete. The self-presentation makes an explicit and more favorable comparison of a speaker's abilities to other individuals.

Ivan Ivanov succeeded in winning a gold medal at the Olympics for lifting a combined weight of 584 pounds. His self-description favorably contrasts his own abilities to those of his competitors.

> I could have lifted more, but my opponents were not so good
> I needed to do more. ("Faces of the Games," 1992, p. 94)

While his actual lifts are impressive, Ivanov claims that he did not need to demonstrate his actual abilities to win the competition. His abilities transcend those of the best competitors in the world.

Other athletes describe their wins as a "cake walk," "a walk in the park," being on "Spring Break," and like a "day off." The athlete makes a comparative appraisal, evaluating his/her own abilities in relationship to others in order to suggest superiority. Although theorists have typically described social comparisons as a technique for determining self-identities, these comparisons are also used to influence other's impressions.

Tellers describe their success as fulfilling a dream. Mary Ellen Clark's career as a diver included several near misses with greatness. In the Olympic qualifiers, she was able to finish second and became the oldest member of the U.S. Diving Team. Her self-presentation communicates her dream to an audience of fans.

> This is a little girl's dream. When this hits me, I will cry, I will lose it . . . All the hard work has finally paid off. My whole family's here, and this is just a dream of everyone's. ("Veteran Wins," 1992, p. 7B)

Her dream is of long-standing, carried from childhood and shared by many people. The success is more significant because it is the realization of an important goal. She also tells fans that reaching the dream required perseverance, simultaneously claiming responsibility and importance.

Dreams are not limited to Olympic hopefuls. Gman Biyik recounts his dream after Cameroon beat Argentina in the first game of the World Cup competition in soccer.

> It was my dream coming here to score the first goal of the tournament, and now it's come true. ("Cameroon Shocks Argentina," 1990, p. 11B)

The goal is realized and the particular athletic accomplishment is promoted to a place of distinction by being connected with the dream.

A dream is an aspiration, a hope that the athlete will be able to secure those successes valued by the sports institution (e.g., winning a medal, participating in a championship). Dreams can be the inspiration for working hard. Sports are closely tied to the American dream:

> Competitive striving, achievement, mobility, and success are major elements of the dominant American Dream ideology in American society. A former athletic director at the University of Southern California indicated the relevance of sport to the American dream when he said, "Athletes develop dedication and a desire to excel in competition, and a realization that success requires hard work." (Nixon, 1984, p. 244)

When an athlete describes a success as the fulfillment of a dream, that person is depicting this particular success as especially desirable. Sports fans are asked to appreciate the significance of the realization of the dream.

How do these enhancement strategies compare to those used by Nobel winners? Athletes display several enhancement strategies absent in Nobel discourse. The only common strategy is the description of obstacles. The nature of the obstacles vary: for athletes, the challenges come from competitors and the limitations of their own bodies; for Nobel winners, the obstacles exist in the complexity of nature. Obstacles have been described in prior research on self-presentation (Giacalone & Riordan, 1990). The association with great individuals in the field is similar to Cialdini's (1989) discussion of basking in reflected glory. While Nobel winners explicitly complimented other scientists, athletes wanted fans to be aware their successes were in the same league with the successes of sports legends. The remaining strategies have not been detected in previous research and are additions to the typology of enhancement strategies. Describing a success as representing the apex of the teller's ability and as unrepeatable are clear attempts to mark the performance as distinctive, meeting an important shared criterion for defining a behavior as a success. Claims of a turning point and supremacy over others reaffirms the overt competitiveness of sports in contrast to the Nobel context. When athletes describe how their successful performance fulfills a dream, they are reenacting cultural values inherent in the idealized American dream. Enhancing the performance by appealing to shared meanings and values within the culture, athletes are able to magnify the significance of their successes.

Success stories make interesting copy, and sportswriters' interviews with winners often generate responses that address entitlement and enhancement of a success. Entitlement strategies build an impression that an athlete's performance is internally caused and controlled. Enhancement strategies magnify the importance of a success and are the most developed in athletes' discourse. In the very competitive world of sports, athletes appear to have developed an extensive repertoire of strategies for presenting a performance in ways that make it look good to fans.

DISCLAIMING DISCOURSE

Modesty is a second goal in telling a success story. Schlenker outlines its importance in self-presentation:

> Modesty is an attractive image. People who are known to be successful but who slightly underplay their strengths and refrain from constantly talking about themselves seem secure, nondefensive, well-adjusted, and pleasant. They don't directly offend others through braggartly, egotistical, or threatening claims. Thus, they are likely to gain social approval and avoid disapproval. (1980, p. 191)

Fans make distinctions between sports heroes who are admired for their successes but remain humble, and bad winners who become arrogant (Vander Velden, 1986). The importance of modesty is captured in slogans found in high school basketball locker rooms (Snyder, 1972): "Talent is God-given; Conceit is self-given;" "There is no I in team." Athletes make explicit reference to the code, praising those who exhibit it and sanctioning those who do not conform. In baseball, Willie McGee approves of players who choose not to boast about their successes.

> I like the way he [Andre Dawson] and [Ryne] Sandberg play. They put up the numbers and they don't talk about it. ("McGee Boosts Average," 1990, p. 13B)

Auto racer Rick Mears prefers modesty and follows the code. He compares his choices with those made by Danny Sullivan.

> He promoted himself [Danny Sullivan] and that was the right way for him. Sometimes I wish I was more like that, but that's not me. It's not what I want to do. I'm afraid that people will think I'm cocky or arrogant. It would make me miserable. I'd rather let my numbers do the talking. (Mulgannon, 1992, p. 56)

The numbers can do the talking because sports successes are factified. Disclaiming discourse attends to the self-presentation of humility and is accomplished by dissociation from responsibility and detraction of the significance of the success.

Dissociation Strategies

An athlete appears modest by making statements that minimize responsibility for the performance. If fans are aware an athlete is responsible, these statements can be interpreted as self-deprecating. In the three strategies for dissociating, tellers (1) attribute success to external or uncontrollable causes, (2) express surprise by the unexpected success or recognition, and (3) share responsibility for the success.

Tellers attribute success to external or uncontrollable causes. When Rex Hudler hit a two-run home run to put the Cardinals ahead seven to three in a 1990 game against the Mets, he describes the connection between bat and ball as serendipitous.

> I'm just happy the ball hit my bat the way it did. ("Cards Sidestep Mets' Comeback," 1990, p. 13B)

The home run is portrayed as the responsibility of the bat and ball and the agent is virtually a spectator to the performance. As an observer, the athlete does not control the cause of the behavior and credit for the success is lessened.

A gold medal on the high bar was the ultimate success for Trent Dimas. He describes his performance as coming together, as if it has an identity apart from the athlete.

> It all came together when I needed it. ("Long Wait Finally Rewarding," 1992, p. 10B)

Instead of saying "I put it all together," an active construction, Dimas says, "It all came together," a passive description of the causal forces. The performance is distanced from the athlete by the use of an impersonal agent. By describing the performance in this way, Dimas appears to attribute the success to an external and uncontrollable force and thus appears modest by disclaiming responsibility for the outcome.

Tellers express surprise at the unexpected success or recognition. Vitaly Scherbo took home six medals in the 1992 Olympic gymnastic competition. His self-presentation emphasizes the unexpected character of the enormous success.

> Well, obviously I am thrilled. I certainly didn't expect that to happen. It seemed to me that it was impossible that I could win so many golds. ("Belorussian Piles Up Gold," 1992, p. 10B)

Surprise is predicated on an unexpected result. That the success is unexpected is a way of asserting the teller is unassuming.

Brian Bonner's success at the Indianapolis 500 auto race led to an opportunity to be A. J. Foyt's apprentice driver. His success comes without warning and is described as difficult to comprehend.

> It's really overwhelming to think about it. To think about the sequence of events and how fast it happened, it's crazy. ("Bonner Still Riding High," 1992, p. 69)

He presents his emotional reaction as one of shock and an inability to fully comprehend what has happened. It is modest to characterize a success as unexpected and to express surprise at its occurrence. This strategy suggests the teller is not arrogant in assuming the success.

Tellers share responsibility for their success. The Chiefs' quarterback, Steve DeBerg, credits the offensive line with an important win over the Raiders in the 1990 season.

> Our offensive line deserves all the credit on the last possession. The Raiders' defensive line was playing great, but our line was up to the task and just took over. I give all the credit

to today's offensive performance to the offensive line. ("KC
Downs Raiders," 1990, p. 11B)

The last possession made the difference in a close game. Although DeBerg could have claimed that his ability to pass 149
yards without interception was the cause for victory, he distributes the credit to his teammates who moved the ball. Particularly in sports requiring interdependence, athletes share credit
with team members (Zaccaro, Peterson, & Walker, 1987).

An emotionally charged finals match between Martina
Navritolva and Zina Garrison netted Martina's first Grand
Slam victory since 1987. Rather than focus on herself, she
allocates credit to others.

> Billie Jean forced me to get my head together and get going.
> Craig's been indispensable. And Judy—she's just always been
> there. I want to thank those guys because they don't get the
> credit they deserve. There are a lot of people out there who
> don't get credit. ("Navratilova Slams Garrison," 1990, p.
> 13B)

She identifies specific individuals and describes their contributions in a complimentary fashion, although the compliment is
couched in terms of its effect on her success.

Sharing credit with others is an act that appears generous
and creates the impression of modesty. The message strategy
disclaims at least partial responsibility and redirects attention
to others who are indirectly associated with the success. Athletes commonly share credit with coaches, family members,
teammates, prior sports heroes, friends, fans, and God.

Dissociation strategies distance a teller of a success story
from responsibility for the success. In attributing success to
external or uncontrollable causes, athletes enact strategies that
are quite similar to excuses in accounts, although the goal is
to appear modest rather than blameless (Schönbach, 1990).
Like Nobel winners, athletes also express surprise at their success
(Miller, Cooke, Tsang, & Morgan, 1992) and share responsibility for the success (Decker, 1987, 1990; Miller, Cooke, Tsang,
& Morgan, 1992).

Detraction Strategies

An athlete can appear modest by depreciating the importance of the success. If the triumph is characterized as less important than an audience may perceive, the sports figure cannot be accused of boasting about its significance. This underplays the importance of the success when the fans are perfectly aware that the athlete is worthy of recognition. Athletes in this study used three detraction strategies, indicating the success was (1) less noteworthy than other accomplishments, (2) incomplete, and (3) flawed.

Tellers note their success is less noteworthy compared to other accomplishments. In a 1990 game against the Kansas City Royals, Gary Gaetti got his 1,200th career hit off Bret Saberhagen. He magnifies his record by associating it with great pitchers, but then he follows it by disparaging the length of time it took him to reach this pinnacle:

> I got my 1,000th hit against Tommy John and my 1,200th hit against Saberhagen, so that's all right. But it took me nine years to get 1,200 hits. Kirby Puckett has that many in about five years. ("Saberhagen Loses," 1990, p. 13B)

While Gaetti is successful, the performance is not as noteworthy as Kirby Puckett's because it took longer. The behavior is not as distinctive as other accomplishments.

Prior to the 1991 World Cup, women's shot put competitions had been dominated by Huang Zhihong. She won the 1989 World Cup with a heave of 68'1/4" and the 1991 World Championship with a throw of 68'41/4". Yet, she chooses to describe her accomplishments modestly:

> Results are results. What I have done is no more newsworthy than if I had swallowed 500 eels. (Lidz, 1992, p. 92)

She downgrades the success by equating it to a less newsworthy performance. Accomplishments in a sporting event should not be perceived as more valuable.

Tellers suggest their success is incomplete. At the end of the second round of the Anheuser-Busch Golf Classic, Morris Hatalsky was five under par and had established a putting record. His self-presentation detracts from the record as a success by focusing on the unfinished tournament.

> That has no significance at all. It really doesn't. All I want to do is have a good tournament. ("Putting Record," 1992, p. 2B)

The success is incomplete because the larger goal of winning the tournament has not been attained. The athlete appears modest by decreasing the significance of the present success in favor of focusing on the future goal.

The American League's coveted Cy Young Award went to Bob Welch in 1990. But the Oakland A's pitcher lost in the World Series to the Cincinnati Reds. The announcement of the award occurred a month after the loss. In Welch's remarks, that unmet goal is still foremost in his talk.

> You'd like to have the other thing, the World Series Championship. ("Welch Clinches," 1990, p. 15B)

The World Series Championship is treated as a more important success than the Cy Young Award. In a team sport, an athlete can appear modest by valuing team success more highly than individual achievement (Zaccaro, Peterson, & Walker, 1987). In directing attention to the incomplete goal, the significance of a particular success is reduced.

Tellers indicate their success is flawed. Kristi Yamaguchi won the gold medal in women's figure skating at the 1992 Winter Olympics. She depicts her successful performance as imperfect.

> I made a major mistake on my triple loop jump. I was surprised I missed it because it's one of my best jumps. I decided to play it safe on my next jump and then go for a strong ending. (Nightingale, 1992, p. 13)

Despite intense training, performances are unpredictable. Yamaguchi missed a jump that is usually among her best. Her winning performance is presented as a performance with a mistake. Fortunately, it is a minor flaw that does not prevent her from winning the gold medal. In describing the error, she reveals her awareness of her imperfections.

Doug Drabek, of the Pittsburgh Pirates, pitched a winning game against the St. Louis Cardinals but disparages his performance because it does not represent his abilities.

> I didn't really have that especially good stuff today; it was just enough to get ahead of people. ("Pirates Beat Cards," 1990, p. 9B)

Although there is a victory, the athlete did not perform at the apex of his abilities. The performance is depreciated by the depiction of the pitching as less than his "best." This strategy, like the enhancement strategy in which tellers describe their performances as representing the apex of their abilities, compares the present performance to an athlete's prior accomplishments.

Even though the athlete has a success story to tell, that athlete's self-presentation is made modest by pointing out that there were errors in the execution or comparing it unfavorably to past performances. The audience understands that these flaws are relatively minor because they do not prevent the athlete from winning. Yet, in calling an audience's attention to them, the sports figure is modest about his or her abilities.

Detraction strategies diminish the success by comparing it to an ideal performance. The strategies of characterizing a success as less noteworthy than other accomplishments and incomplete are also evident in Nobel prize winners' discourse. Athletes further detract from their successes by pointing to the flaws in their performance, providing a new strategy to add to the developing typology.

Tellers of these success stories engage in disclaiming discourse to avoid appearing to be bad winners. They dissociate themselves from responsibility for the success and detract from the importance of the success. While there is overlap in the strategies employed by athletes and Nobel laureates, this application has added two additional disclaiming strategies.

Athletes are prominent tellers of success stories. They shape attributions about their successes through acclaiming and disclaiming discourse. In their stories, they are the winners and winning is essential.

> There is nothing quite like it. Win hands down, win going away, win by accident, win by a nose, win without deserving it. Winning is the tops. Winning is what it's all about. Winning is the be-all and end-all, and don't let anybody tell you otherwise. All the world loves a winner. (Roth, 1973)

4

Cosmetic Queens in Pink Cadillacs:
Recasting Women's Success in Mary Kay Cosmetics

On a rainy Monday night in September, women in professional dress and carefully applied faces arrive for a Mary Kay Success Meeting. Their arrivals are punctuated by excited exchanges about the week they had selling Mary Kay. The director, Cathy, greets every woman, dispensing advice and encouragement. She exudes confidence, attired in a stylish, pink Director's suit designating her elevated position in Mary Kay Inc. On the lapel, a large gold bumblebee nestles among four rows of diamond pins proclaiming the hundreds of thousands of dollars of sales production by her unit, "Cathy's Comets," for the last four years.

Cathy opens the Success Meeting with an enthusiastic, "Good evening," and the audience of distributors and guests reciprocate the greeting. She replies, "You can do better than that!" The audience roars, "Good evening," to Cathy's obvious approval.

She introduces the "best management team" in Lewistown, and three women stride up the middle aisle to join her in front. Consultants clap and cheer the "red jackets," Mary Kay Inc. middle management. Women earn the right to wear a red jacket when they recruit at least three business associates to the company. Cathy asks these successful women to share why they chose Mary Kay. Sarah replies that Mary Kay is "fun and you get to meet neat people and make lots of friends." Her remarks rouse enthusiastic applause. Kelly, a recent red jacket, divulges that she likes sitting at the head table and drinking iced tea, two privileges reserved for red jackets. Laughter mingles with applause. Tina praises the opportunity for growth in Mary Kay and insists it is available to each of the women present. Fervent applause follows. The red jackets take their place at the head table.

Tonight, twenty-seven women sit behind rows of tables facing Cathy and the head table of red jackets in the conference room of a large hotel. Cathy's Comets are predominantly Caucasian, middle-class women with professional training or some college education, in their mid thirties and forties. They attend tonight's meeting after having worked a full day as nurses, dieticians, elementary school teachers, real estate agents, clerical and administrative personnel, waitresses, and home-makers. Attendance at Mary Kay Success Meetings is not required (although it is strongly encouraged and considered instrumental to success), so that on any given Monday, there are the regulars who rarely miss a meeting, returning distributors who surface intermittently, new recruits who are still in training, and guests who are potential Mary Kay Inc. recruits. Each consultant introduces herself and her guests and receives applause. Some women report how long they have been in Mary Kay, an exciting accomplishment that occurred during the week (recruiting a new business associate, teaching a particularly successful class), or warmly introduce a guest. Ten minutes into the meeting, every woman in the room has been recognized and applauded.

New business associates are welcomed into the Mary Kay unit through an initiation ritual. Cathy asks June, a consultant with the company for nearly a year, and Carrie, June's first recruit and one of the few African American women present, to come forward. As Cathy attaches a Mary Kay pin to Carrie's blouse, she advises her to wear it everywhere because people will approach her who no longer have a consultant or who are interested in the Mary Kay opportunity. Cathy turns to the audience and asks if this has happened to any of them recently and four women immediately raise their hands to confirm the wisdom of her advice. The audience is attentive as June hands

Carrie a single red rose while Cathy intones, "Mary Kay says that when you join the company you're like a tiny rosebud and the longer you're in the company, the more you blossom and grow and become the woman God intended you to be." Cathy and June warmly embrace Carrie, and they all bestow wide smiles on an appreciative audience. Carrie is asked to share why she joined the company and she reveals, "June has been a wonderful influence on me. Both June and Cathy were very important in my decision. I was impressed with Mary Kay and decided I would love to be a part of Mary Kay." There is approving applause. Carrie is now part of the Mary Kay unit and her success will contribute to the group's success.

The atmosphere is electric as Cathy begins to recognize distributors for weekly accomplishments. She retrieves a large stack of vividly colored ribbons and calls out Bev's name. Bev has been a Mary Kay Inc. consultant for four years and needs just one more recruit to become a red jacket. She receives ribbons for a $425 class, a $150 facial, and a $575 week. The audience applauds and admires Bev's accomplishments. Ten others are individually recognized, and those receiving multiple ribbons or producing exceptionally high sales merit extra commendation. The audience claps and cheers when Cathy queries, "Isn't that great?" and briefly embraces each woman. Consultants are socialized to express joy untinged by envy for other's successes as they contribute to the achievements of the group and motivate individual accomplishments.

Women eligible for a bar pin take center stage. Two women come forward while the director retrieves a box of faux diamond pins declaring personal sales since the last Seminar, the national Mary Kay extravaganza. The numbered pins are in $1000 increments. Tina, an effusive red jacket who wants to follow in Cathy's footsteps, trades for a $3000 pin, while Amy, a consultant contemplating quitting her nursing job to do Mary Kay full time, receives the $2000 pin Tina relinquished and is ecstatic because it "is obviously lucky." The audience shows appreciation for these accomplishments by clapping loudly and offering congratulatory comments as each woman collects a new pin and a hug from Cathy.

Cathy begins an eagerly anticipated Success Meeting ritual as she asks each woman who "worked her business" this week to stand. Virtually all of the distributors stand. She asks those who sold $100 during the week to remain standing and five women sit down. Cathy asks those who sold $200 to remain standing and four more women take their seats. The audience holds its breath and expresses admiration as the numbers climb and there are three women still standing at $600. These women are invited to the front amid boisterous applause. They line up, smiling broadly, and Cathy continues the countdown. "Seven hundred dollars?" Two of the women step back, leaving Lois in the spotlight. Lois is a receptionist who was recruited by Tina less than a year ago. Cathy asks whether Lois sold "Eight hundred?" She grins and nods her head. "Nine hundred? One thousand dollars?" And she nods again. Women in the audience are impressed, and Lois reports excitedly that she sold $1010 in a week. Thunderous clapping marks her extraordinary success. Cathy asks her to tell the others how she was successful, and Lois describes the number of hours she worked and her commitment to hold several classes. Cathy shows the audience the "beautiful pin" she awards Lois for top sales of the week. There is another round of applause and Cathy gives each of the women a hug before they return to their seats.

Cathy summons women forward who have earned a bumblebee. The bumblebee is a symbol of achievement, for, as Mary Kay Ash, the founder of Mary Kay Inc., says, engineers can't explain why a creature with small wings and a heavy body can still fly. Mary Kay consultants are reminded they are just as capable of such feats. A bumblebee pin is given to distributors who successfully complete a weekly challenge. Three women come to the front of the room and receive bumblebee pins, hugs from Cathy, and applause from the other consultants. Bev is singled out for additional praise because she consistently challenges herself to "step out of her comfort zone" to confront her fears.

This evening Cathy chooses to share an inspirational message drawn from an article appearing in the *Director's Memo*, a weekly newsletter for sales directors from the national office.

In it, a Mary Kay director from another state declares the importance of a sense of humor in training consultants, conducting classes, and living life. To illustrate, she tells the story of eating candy at a skin care class and discovering it had been a dog treat. Then there was the time she taught a class where "cockroaches were doing the backstroke in a sink of dirty dishes." The distributors in Cathy's Comets listen attentively and laugh at the author's comic experiences. In summarizing the article, Cathy suggests consultants learn to enjoy their Mary Kay classes and recognize they help customers feel good about themselves with Mary Kay products. The audience nods and smiles in agreement.

Weekly summary sheets report sales and Cathy rewards those who turn them in by drawing for a prize. Martha, a consultant of less than a year who used to find the applause and hugs discomfiting, is the winner. But now, Martha is delighted with the attention and confides she never won anything before. Cathy bestows a large heart pin, and they exchange hugs to applause.

A raffle drawing for women attending the Success Meeting is next. The prize is a much coveted, sequined evening bag, and the winner is Trish, a new consultant with plans to quit her real estate job to do Mary Kay full time. She is excited and quickly collects her prize.

In closing, Cathy reminds each woman to "give at least two hugs before leaving because every woman needs at least eight hugs a day." The women linger, breaking into small groups to talk about the awards won this week, the upcoming Mary Kay events, the products they need to trade. Most of the regulars continue these discussions in the hotel restaurant over a late-evening snack. When they part, they are primed to have a great Mary Kay week.

The desire for success is pervasive in our culture and reaffirmed in the preceding description of an important Mary Kay event, the weekly Success Meeting. I chose Mary Kay Cosmetics because it was a promising site for observing discourse about women's success. In 1963, Mary Kay Ash used her personal savings to establish Mary Kay Cosmetics. By 1992, 300,000 distributors in twenty-one countries had produced sales of $613 million (Farnham, 1993). Mary Kay Inc. is listed among the Fortune 500, ranked in the top ten companies best for women, and boasts that 70 percent of the women earning over $50,000 a year are working for Mary Kay ("In the Pink," 1993; January 26 interview with June). There are seventy-four Mary Kay millionaires (having earned $1 million or more in commissions) and thousands of Mary Kay directors driving pink Cadillacs, the company's well-known "trophy on wheels." "Cathy's Comets," the Mary Kay unit I observed, had been repeatedly recognized at Seminar as a Top Unit. It was directed by a woman who drove a pink Cadillac, qualified for lavish top director trips, had offspring directors in several states with nearly a thousand distributors in her area (the unit that met in Lewistown as well as all other units of offspring directors), and intended to be a national sales director, the highest position in the company.

METHOD

My initial attempts to examine acclaiming and disclaiming discourse were stymied by the complexity of the meanings of success negotiated among members of the Mary Kay culture. Economic success was obvious, but there were other forms of success. Even economic success appeared to be more than the simple acquisition of wealth. Before I could describe acclaiming and disclaiming discourse about success, I needed to problematize the concept of success. This chapter addresses how success is socially construed and negotiated in Mary Kay.

I observed weekly Mary Kay Success Meetings of Cathy's Comets for five months and conducted extensive interviews with thirteen women who were members of this Mary Kay unit. Field notes from these observations and transcripts of the interviews were supplemented by materials produced by the national office and the director (e.g., newsletters, magazines, video recruiting tapes, advertisements, Mary Kay's autobiography). Member-checking procedures were used to verify factual details and solicit feedback about the conceptual framework. In this chapter, I offer an interpretation of the meaning of success derived from the constant comparison method: creating categories for meanings of success, characterizing the properties of each category, and integrating the categories in a theoretical framework (Glaser & Strauss, 1967; Strauss, 1990). The categories I generated for meanings of success include prosperity as success, status as success, and personal transformation as success. I argue that women's success stories are constrained by cultural expectations and are recast as understandable cultural narratives (Rosenwald & Ochberg, 1992). The appendix provides additional methodological details.

ANALYSIS

PROSPERITY AS SUCCESS

"There were three things that attracted me to Mary Kay: money, money, and money!" declares Joanne enthusiastically as she recounts why she chose Mary Kay (November 22 Success Meeting). And, at the meeting described at the beginning of this chapter, Lois is praised for selling $1010 in Mary Kay products in a week. In this section, I depict the first definition of success: the acquisition of wealth through Mary Kay sales and recruiting. But success discourses by women are constrained by cultural expectations (Banks & Zimmerman, 1987; Gergen, 1992). In particular, I propose that prosperity is redefined as an act of caring and an affirmation of the priority of family. This reframing of the meaning of prosperity makes the success story of Mary Kay distributors more understandable and acceptable.

Money and Mary Kay

Money, the symbol of prosperity, tops the agenda at weekly Success Meetings. As distributors introduce themselves, they excitedly report and receive recognition for weekly financial accomplishments.

> Simone introduces herself and explains she has been in Mary Kay for four years. She tells the others how she was delivering a Day Radiance [a foundation retailing for $10] and took a basket [of Mary Kay products] with her and another woman bought $150! The audience applauds. (November 15 Success Meeting)[1]

Simone made money by selling Mary Kay. A distributor begins with a 50% profit so others can easily calculate that Simone earned $75 in this brief transaction. That the sale is unexpected augments its value.

The introductions are a precursor for a significant and routine episode, the presentation of weekly awards in Success Meetings. Ribbons for sales, pearls and spacers for selling basic sets (a collection of skin care products with a retail value of $40 or more), bar pins (for total sales since Seminar), and top sales (the highest weekly award according to most of the women interviewed) are all recognitions of distributors who made money through Mary Kay.

The dramatic ritual for awarding top sales, in particular, accords importance to economic success. Suspense builds as the sales figures climb and the number of women standing decreases to ultimately reveal the person with the highest sales for another week.

> Cathy asks who worked their Mary Kay business this week? Most of the consultants and red jackets stand. There is applause and Bev and Tina call out "Woo! Woo! Woo!" Cathy asks who did $100? Everyone is still standing. There is applause. $200? Only four women remain. The applause is louder. $300? The same four are still standing. There is more applause. $400? $500? They all sit down. Cathy asks them

to come to the front. They line up where everyone can see them and Cathy asks them how much they sold during the week. The highest is $432.50. Cathy asks each consultant to tell the others how they had such a GREAT week, beginning with the person with the highest sales. Martha says she had a big class, another class, and a facial. She advises those in the audience to talk to everyone about the Mary Kay opportunity. Martha believes her success is due to her consistency. Cathy responds, "Good job!" and gives her a hug. The distributors in the audience applaud. Tina, a red jacket, says she had two facials, a class, and reorders. Cathy says, "Good," and gives her a hug. The audience applauds. Simone tells the others she sold two basic nail cares and had two reorders. Cathy responds positively and gives her a hug. Applause follows. Amy says her sales were reorders and skin revival systems. She gets a hug from Cathy and applause from the audience. Cathy lets Martha pick either a Mary Kay notebook or a pink garment bag as the prize for high sales. Martha picks the garment bag and she receives congratulatory comments from others as she returns to her seat. (October 11 Success Meeting)

Winning high sales proclaims to the members of the unit that this woman sold a remarkable sum in products. June confirms that when a consultant has "a high week, then everybody is impressed" (October 26 Interview). Cathy, Martha, and the audience collaborate in producing success discourse that acclaims and celebrates economic success. The winner of this award is accorded the position of a privileged narrator, invited to share her success strategies with others. When it is Martha's turn, she advises the group that monetary success is the result of consistency and recruiting.

Achieving prosperity through Mary Kay is reaffirmed as cause for celebration in monthly newsletters from Cathy. The front page of the September newsletter proclaims, "Check out these winners!" It includes photographs of women identified as the monthly "queens of recruiting, sales, wholesale, facial sales, phone sales, and most classes held." The dollar amounts and the number of recruits and bookings are prominent. Another page, with the heading "Success in Action" lists women who had "wonderful weeks" or earned places in the $2000, $1500, $500, and $400 unit clubs. The back of this page includes the names of distributors and dollar amounts for "phone sales, super sales, fabulous facials, and classy classes." Sprinkled among these figures are motivational statements, such as "We're rising to the top!" and "You're awesome!" Distributors also receive *Applause*, a monthly magazine from the company. A regular feature is a list of unit sales production totals and the income earned in commissions by top directors and national sales directors.

Yearly successes are celebrated at Seminar, the ultimate Mary Kay event where 36,000 consultants descend on Dallas for what is commonly described as a "cross between a Broadway production, Miss America, and Queen for a Day" (October 21 interview with Tina). Top earners appear in Queen's Courts, secure the privilege of having lunch with Mary Kay Ash, and are awarded "Cinderella gifts" of cars, furs, jewelry, and vacation trips. Those who are making money by selling and recruiting are lavishly rewarded with symbols of wealth.

The Mary Kay culture is peopled with the "rags to riches" stories of top performers, adopting the narrative form of a progressive story, where individuals tell how they became who they are by leaving behind what they were (Freccero, 1986). Mary Kay Ash's story is one that every distributor seems to know. She wanted to be a doctor but her parents couldn't afford to send her to college. She married and divorced, becoming financially responsible for her family. Mary Kay took a sales position with Stanley Home Products and had to borrow $12 to attend the sales convention, but was the Queen of Sales the next year. She trained salespeople at another company and watched men become more successful. When she retired, Mary Kay invested her meager personal savings in Mary Kay Cosmetics (Ash, 1987; Fucini & Fucini, 1985) to give women an opportunity to excel. Now, Mary Kay Ash heads a multimillion dollar business (Farnham, 1993).

Economic success also figures prominently in the narratives imparted about other successful women in Mary Kay Inc.

> She's a National Sales Director. She's really overcome many things in her life. She's really a remarkable person. She started out—when she started to do Mary Kay she was on welfare. And she was in government housing. And she saved up her money so she could buy the kit. And now she's a National Sales Director earning maybe—I don't know how much. In our *Applause* magazine, it tells how much her checks are. And I think hers—I may be wrong but I think hers are maybe $18,000 a month. (October 5 interview with Simone)

Simone's retelling of this national sales director's story recounts a dramatic struggle against poverty. The evidence of victory is monetary. That five other Mary Kay consultants volunteered this woman's story on different occasions suggests its importance within the culture.

On another occasion, Sarah, an active red jacket, relates a success story about a Mary Kay director who is making a lot of money.

> She was like over 200 pounds working like in an Amoco station. And she'd been fired from some kind of job and they told her she didn't know how to manage money—to handle the money. And she's been in the company for four years and she went from a $450,000 director to a million dollar director in one year. She was 28 years old. (October 26 interview with Sarah)

Sarah tells the story of a woman who worked at an unappealing minimum wage job and was fired because she couldn't handle money. Her meteoric rise in Mary Kay to a million dollar director (with obvious financial rewards) is ironic given the prior judgment that she could not handle money. The telling and retelling of progressive stories about Mary Kay role models depict struggles against economic foes and victory in economic terms.

Prosperity as success is publicly affirmed and reaffirmed in the Mary Kay culture. Mary Kay distributors validate this meaning of success by acclaiming economic accomplishments and praising women to prosperity through applause and awards.

In the valued role of the storyteller, women share their personal success stories and pass on meaningful advice to those who seek to emulate their monetary success. Their names and stories are celebrated in Mary Kay publications. The heroines of success stories retold by distributors leave poverty behind to become prosperous through Mary Kay.

Redefining the Success Story about Prosperity

Success is defined within cultural stories of achievement. As discussed in chapter 1, the romance as a narrative form (Frye, 1957) pits the hero against obstacles, but the outcome is ultimately happy. Campbell (1956) argued that most narratives are variations on a monomyth, testing the protagonist with personal and historical obstacles. Narrative form and content are expressions of ideology, "representations by which we construct and accept values and institutions" (DuPlessis, 1985, p. x). Stories are rendered understandable because they reflect this ideology.

Cultural stories about achievement situate heroes as committed to a singular purpose, overcoming obstacles, and ultimately achieving victory. But heroines typically play minor roles as love interests (Jelinek, 1980; DuPlessis, 1985), so that "of all the possible actions people can do in fiction, very few can be done by women" (Russ, 1972, p. 4).

Autobiographies reflect differences in the content and form of nonfiction success stories. In the autobiographies of men, careers are "central lines of narrative structuring, and personal commitments, external to their careers, are relegated to insignificant plots," while careers in the narratives of women are "not an ultimate end point" (Jelinek, 1980, pp. 134–135). Women's achievements are embedded in their connectedness to others and their personal identities (Gergen, 1992).

The protagonists celebrated in "rags to riches" stories are usually men. Historically, women acquired wealth at the pleasure of their husbands or fathers. As the percentage of working women increased, they were presumably in a position to acquire personal wealth through their own business interests. Despite their numbers, cultural narratives about women's business successes and the attendant accumulation of personal wealth are uncommon (Fucini & Fucini, 1985; Macksey & Macksey, 1975). The relative absence of this discourse is due in part to the fact that there are fewer woman stories to tell manifesting economic success. Women work in the "pink ghetto." sixty-two percent are employed in female-dominated occupations that are largely underpaid. On the average, women are earning only 72 percent of the income earned by men in the same occupations (Harris, 1995). Nonetheless, some women become prosperous, but their stories may redefine the meaning of prosperity. To be intelligible within the culture, women tell a different story, for "even when women are leaders in their professions, or exceptional in some arena of life, they find it difficult to tell their personal narratives in the forms that would be suitable to their male colleagues" (Gergen, 1992, p. 131).

In Mary Kay, women can become wealthy by selling cosmetics and recruiting others to the company. There are 74 Mary Kay millionaires, and national sales directors routinely earn in excess of $200,000 a year. Cathy's estimated earnings this year exceed $100,000 (based on commission figures appearing in *Applause*). Mary Kay distributors have success stories to tell that are about economic achievements. However, their stories are recast by defining prosperity as acts of caring and affirmations of the priority of family. Money is not simply an end but is clearly and extensively redefined as a means to other ends.

Acts of caring. Mary Kay distributors conduct "classes" and hold "demonstrations" rather than "sell products." Tina, a committed red jacket, corrects her cousin's misperception.

> Tina reports that her cousin asked her over the weekend how long she had been *selling* Mary Kay Cosmetics. Tina reacted immediately: "I've been *giving skin care classes* for 2½ years." (September 13 Success Meeting)

By providing instruction, nurturance, and quality products that "make women feel better about themselves," sales are transformed from a sordid economic transaction into a higher purpose: helping others (Biggart, 1989). Elizabeth, a red jacket, explains to consultants that selling Mary Kay allows you to have a positive influence on client's lives:

> It's building other women's self-esteems. It is being able to make women glow. (October 25 Success Meeting)

Dana describes a difficult facial. Her client had initially been uncooperative but she is thrilled with the results.

> It made me really happy to make someone else happy and confident in her appearance. Mary Kay is a good company. It makes you feel good about you and that can be reflected in someone else. It makes other people feel good. (November 15 Success Meeting)

By teaching other women how to become confident in appearance, the act of making money is exemplary and distanced from competitive and self-interested motivations. This redefinition gives women permission to be prosperous. Mary Kay Ash characterizes the relationship promoted between people and profit: "Our belief in caring for people, however, does not conflict with our need as a corporation to generate a profit. Yes, we keep our eye on the bottom line, but it's not an overriding obsession. To me, P and L doesn't only mean profit and loss—it also means people and love" (Ash, 1984, p. xix). Distributors "conceptualize their Mary Kay experience—recruiting and selling—as giving" (Waggoner, 1994, p. 74). They see their sales interactions "in ways that do not do violence to their sense of themselves as women" (Biggart, 1989, p. 97) and that makes their stories of prosperity intelligible to themselves and the culture.

Affirming the priority of family. Man stories are dominated by career plot lines with personal relationships at the periphery, while women's cultural narratives situate their relationships with others and their personal identities as prevailing story lines (Gergen, 1992; Jelinek, 1980). Successful men can delegate family responsibilities to women or define their role as the "breadwinner," but prosperous women are expected to simultaneously excel in sustaining the family. An understandable story of a prosperous woman suggests that Mary Kay earnings benefit the family and she did not neglect her family responsibilities.

The act of selling is a means to nurture family. A successful Mary Kay distributor has the ability to provide material signs of affection. For Melanie, that affection took the form of a car that could be shared with her husband and a college education for her children.

> I told my husband I could win a car in Mary Kay and now I can give him a lift. We needed Mary Kay to put kids through nine years of college! (November 22 Success Meeting)

The profits earned through Mary Kay provide material goods for families; earning money for others is a symbolic display of affection. A director declares: "I know that I'm going to be able to give my family everything I feel they deserve" ("Discover for Yourself," 1992, p. 3). When their earnings help their families, making money becomes acceptable and praiseworthy.

The motto, "God first, family second, career third" is heard at every Success Meeting and is quoted often in Mary Kay publications. Distributors are encouraged to "get their priorities straight," and many I interviewed suggest that this pervasive attitude was important in their decision to get involved in Mary Kay. In Mary Kay Inc., a woman can be prosperous *and* maintain her family responsibilities.

Mary Kay Cosmetics offers an alternative to traditional work. The company presents itself as more responsive to the needs of families than traditional work arrangements. Cathy stresses this point as she talks with a group of potential recruits.

> Mary Kay allows flexibility. You can take a day off when you want to take a day off. You can spend time with your children. You can be there when they get home from school. You can be there on Saturday mornings when they want you to be at home. (October 25 Success Meeting)

The contrast between Mary Kay Cosmetics and positions where women can earn comparable incomes is based on preserving the priority of family.

> Executive women think they're making tons of money at $50,000 and $100,000 a year. But they're stressed out and they never see their families because they're working 18 hours a day. I also love the fact that I can financially contribute to my family and still pick up my kids at school! ("Dare to Dream," 1993, p. 7)

Mary Kay women can be prosperous and have time for their families.

Mary Kay distributors in Cathy's Comets envision abandoning full time, wage positions for a prosperous future that privileges family before career:

> I had a great week! My husband says if I keep it up I can quit my job! (September 13 Success Meeting)

Women can tell a success story about prosperity that is compatible with cultural narratives because their connectedness to others (i.e., the family) is preserved.

In summary, within this Mary Kay unit, women are recognized for making money. The earnings of top performers are proclaimed and women are rewarded with symbols of wealth for economic achievements. Prosperity is valued in the narratives told by and about Mary Kay distributors, in the publications of sales figures, in the descriptions of weekly monetary successes, in the awards presented at Success Meetings, and in the aspirations of Mary Kay distributors. Banks and Zimmerman (1987) argue that the corporate ideology of Mary Kay Inc. encourages women to seek economic prosperity without challenging male financial privilege.

> Mary Kay's discursive strategies reinforce the sexual division of labor in the family. Through Mary Kay, a housewife's labor within the exchange market that the company creates and controls, is not only framed as "teaching," "consulting," and "expertise," but is simultaneously positioned as a service for a more luxurious maintenance of the family. (p. 90)

Women's success discourse is constrained by cultural expectations. Prosperity as the meaning of success is made understandable by redefining prosperity as an act of caring and providing for family.

STATUS AS SUCCESS

> Cathy warmly welcomes Tammy, a Mary Kay Director from another unit. Tammy shares her "I" story, beginning by explaining that women didn't have many opportunities when she first started working. She was employed by a bank and eventually became a Vice President. But she quit corporate America because it was rigid, failed to praise her, and imposed a glass ceiling. In Mary Kay, she became a Director, earned a pink car, and was making the same money within a year. She moves closer to the audience, making direct eye contact with several consultants, declaring, "YOU can go where you want in Mary Kay. There is no stopping you!" The audience of distributors listens carefully and applauds eagerly. (October 11 Success Meeting)

Tammy's story suggests her experience is not unique, that anyone can be successful in Mary Kay. The Protestant work ethic merges with meritocracy, "the idea that status and social rewards are distributed according to individual accomplishment" (Biggart, 1989, p. 106), not inherited characteristics.

Unlike more traditional businesses, status in Mary Kay cannot be purchased. For Fran, an ambitious but more mature Mary Kay consultant of only four months, it is of some import that success (achieving the status of a director) is not determined by age, natural beauty, or education:

> Because I look in the *Applause* magazine and I see women that are directors that look like they're 25 or 30 and they're beautiful. And I see other women that are plain unattractive. Yet they're a director too. So that's what's so wonderful. And some of them are 20 and some of them are 60. This is what excites me is that at my age I can still have an opportunity to become, you know, a director of the company and be as

successful as someone with a college degree that's 25 years old. (November 11 interview)

Fran's aspirations to become a director display her sense that status is earned.

This section on status as success describes the manifestations of status conferred by members of the Mary Kay community at the four levels in the hierarchy: (1) beauty consultants, (2) red jackets, (3) directors, and (4) national sales directors. Status and prosperity are interdependent. A distributor earns higher commissions as she advances in the Mary Kay hierarchy. I argue that Mary Kay distributors in Cathy's Comets are able to produce understandable status discourse because they have feminized the meaning of status by tying it to cooperation rather than competition, and they have situated their own status within a hierarchy traditionally dominated by men.

The Hierarchy in Mary Kay

Beauty consultants. In the Mary Kay hierarchy, everyone starts at the same place, with a minimum order of $600 in wholesale products from the company. Beauty consultants are at the lowest level. They are the primary audience for "I" stories told by women who have more status, earn the smallest percentage in commissions, and attend training sessions. At Success Meetings, they are seated in a large group and drink ice water provided in the back of the room. What status they have is derived from having committed themselves to Mary Kay Cosmetics.

Red jackets. The "red jackets" wear a red blazer, sit at the head table, drink iced tea, tell their "I" stories, offer advice to beauty consultants, and earn a percentage of their recruit's commissions. At the Success Meeting described in the introduction, Cathy introduces the "best management team" in Lewistown and invites Sarah, Kelly, and Tina to describe why they chose Mary Kay. A woman initially belongs to this select group when she recruits three active business associates. Those who earn the rank quickly are respected because recruiting is considered more difficult than selling. As I interviewed women at various ranks in Cathy's Comets, I asked who was successful in the group. "Red jackets" were mentioned more frequently than consultants. Consultants aspire to be red jackets. Jill, who works as a waitress in her other job, identifies moving to this rank as a short-term goal.

> My short-term goals are "Being a red jacket soon so I can start getting my commission checks." (October 22 interview)

A woman advances to team leader when she recruits five active members and then she can wear a special pin on the lapel of her red jacket and earn more in commissions. Team leaders become team managers when they have twelve members, maintain $4000 wholesale for four consecutive months, and earn a red Grand Am. During my observations, Tina was in "car production," and Cathy routinely introduced her at Success Meetings as an "On-Target Team Manager," reporting the number of months the team had reached the required production. Consistent with Cathy's commendation, Tina was named frequently as the most successful Mary Kay distributor in the interviews. Tina's depiction of her accomplishment considers the recognition provided by others as well as reporting the prestige achieved for having accomplished her present rank quickly.

> My major accomplishment was to get my red jacket and those first recruits. And I have never in my entire life had such a sense of feeling that night. I told—it was like that I guess I had five recruits because I had gone on target for my car. It was like the first five came very steady. Like within a month. And that night at the meeting I had my red jacket on and everybody went around the room and applauded me and gave me a standing ovation. And I thought, "Gosh, I did this myself." (October 21 interview)

A team manager displays her rank by wearing a scarf with a key design with her red blazer and driving a red company Grand Am. The *Applause* magazine's publication of VIP car winners each month is another indication of the status accorded the company for this rank.

Directors. A woman may qualify to be considered for the position of director by earning the rank of team manager or by building an equivalent team and accumulating substantial personal and recruit sales. When she has thirty recruits, she forms her own unit and becomes an offspring of her director. Tina visualizes accomplishing this rank.

> *Q:* Now tell me what happens when you become a Director? Then does that—do the people you recruited become your own—their own unit?

> *Tina:* What will happen—see I'm talking the present tense here—is that I will start having my own unit meetings. OK? And I have to recruit twelve personal recruits, meaning people that I bring in to the company by myself. And the Director should always keep recruiting. OK? But a minimum of twelve. After I have the twelve, I earn the car. That's why I'm saying I've got to get four recruits by the end of October. Then my recruits can recruit. And the twelve can recruit and that builds a unit of thirty. You have to have a minimum of thirty for a unit. And then we'll build on that and start having unit meetings. (October 21 interview)

The larger the size of the unit, the more capacity it has to produce sales and continue recruiting efforts that add to the prestige accorded its director.

Directors are queens in Mary Kay. They debut at Seminar before thousands of applauding consultants who dream of being in their place one day. They meet Mary Kay personally at director's training. A director's status is designated by a tailored, designer director's suit. Cathy proudly wears this year's pink director's suit at most Success Meetings. Simone, a beauty consultant who recently made the decision to do Mary Kay full time, explains that directors are identifiable by their appearance and held in awe because "you realize what each one has had to do to get that accomplished to wear that suit. I mean it's really very impressive" (October 5 interview).

Directors of units with high sales production are awarded pink Buick Regals and Cadillacs at Seminar. The pink cars are a status symbol for a director and her unit, for "beauty consultants consider it a mark of prestige to be in a 'pink car unit' and work hard to help the director earn one" (Biggart, 1989, p. 152). As I arrived at Success Meetings during the observations, Cathy's pink Cadillac was always prominently parked at the front door. Like many others, June, working toward her "red jacket," dreams of obtaining this symbol of success.

Q: What does a pink car signify?

June: It signifies that I've been successful when I started in this company. Yeah, I want to get into a pink car. I would just do anything. But now, you know, I want a pink Cadillac. At Seminar, I just I kind of try to foresee it. (October 26 interview)

Directors receive special publications from the company, their sales production figures are listed in the monthly magazine, their success stories are told in *Applause* and newsletters, they earn an increased commission on the sales production of their unit, and they set the agenda at Success Meetings. Directors are cheerleaders, motivators, trainers, advisors, arbitrators, and gentle critics for a team of distributors. A multiplicity of roles and messages within a complex layering of status symbols designate the lofty position of directors within the organization.

A director's status "is measured in part by the number of offspring a woman gives birth to" (Biggart, 1989, p. 85). A senior director has at least one offspring director, while an executive senior director has at least five active offspring directors. Each wears a blouse of a different color with the director's suit to designate rank. The growth of offspring directors is accompanied by an increase in monthly commissions earned by the original director. Status is thus entwined with prosperity. While the director is perceived as genuinely interested in the personal success of each member of the unit (altruism before personal gain), "higher levels of status and income can come about only with the success of the downline" (Biggart, 1989, p. 19).

National sales directors.   The highest rank in Mary Kay is national sales director. A woman must have at least twelve first-line offspring directors or ten first-line directors, eight of whom must be senior directors. National sales directors wear a distinct designer suit and are eligible for enormous bonuses and a generous retirement program. Their pictures adorn the walls at Mary Kay Inc. headquarters and Mary Kay Cosmetics publishes a volume containing the "I" success stories of the national sales directors. Their monthly commission earnings are proclaimed in *Applause.*

The status of national sales directors is promulgated by the respect granted and the desire to achieve this level by women working their way up the hierarchy. Being a national sales director is perceived as being at the very top.

> *Q:* What do you think it means to be successful?

> *Sarah:* That's [being a National] like the epitome of everybody in Mary Kay. Because more money, and you have more people under you and you know that's the top of our company. To be a National. I want to be a National. I want all the perks. I want all the everything. In order to do that you become a National. (October 12 interview)

National sales directors are the embodiment of success. In Cathy's Comets, there was a great deal of excitement because Cathy announced her goal of advancing to the rank of a national sales director in the next year.

Redefining the Success Story about Status

Cultural narratives about the acquisition of status in the business environment often depict a man clawing his way to the top. Few are promoted to the summit, and a keen competitive edge is necessary for advancement and retention of these positions (Steinberg, 1984). Women are constrained from telling this story about their acquisition of status. In Mary Kay Cosmetics, women redefine success discourses about status by feminizing the meaning of status within the culture and by positioning their status within the dominant male hierarchy.

Feminizing status. The process of acquiring status is feminized. A woman becomes successful through cooperation rather than competition. "They [Mary Kay distributors] sometimes discourage even friendly competition among distributors, promoting a 'go-give' spirit, not a 'go-get' attitude" (Biggart, 1989, p. 5). An indication of the devaluation of internal competition is a rule that prescribes that no one should steal another distributor's customer or potential recruit. Fran explains that while distributors are anxious to succeed, they must abide by this rule.

> She [a guest Fran asked to a Mary Kay meeting] told me that evening after we were done with the facial that she had been facialed by two other consultants right there in my unit and that both of them had been trying to get her to join the company so I backed off immediately. Because that's the company's philosophy and I believe in that. And I said, "I appreciate you coming and being my guest" and she bought a couple of small little items and I said, "But I realize you're another consultant's customer and I honor that." (November 11 interview)

While distributors gain their status by selling and recruiting, they are discouraged from competing with other women in their unit. Cooperation rather than competition is seen as the process for acquiring status. The emphasis on cooperation feminizes the meaning of status as possible through cooperation rather than competition and makes success discourse about status more understandable as a woman's story of success.

Status within the dominant hierarchy.   A status success story
can be told by women in Mary Kay Cosmetics because it does
not challenge the dominant male hierarchy. The four levels of
status in Mary Kay Inc. described in this section essentially
differentiate some women from other women. The five member board of directors is dominated by male executives. Mary
Kay Ash is the chairman emeritus and Amy DiGeso heads the
international division (Whiddon, April 25, 1996). Mary Kay
Ash explains that men occupy the top corporate positions
because her son administers the company and naturally chooses
male assistants and that "we couldn't pay our representatives
enough to give up their freedom" (Rockman, 1980, p. 38).
Women's success occurs within the confines of women's hierarchies and values.

   In addition, women's positions within women's hierarchies
do not encroach on traditional status roles within families.

> Direct selling organizations, even one led by such an obvious
> booster of women as Mary Kay Ash, do not challenge the
> prevailing sociopolitical arrangements of society. In fact, it is
> probably the compromise direct selling represents that has
> made it attractive to so many women. They can be person-
> ally empowered—feel liberated and modern—without upset-
> ting the traditional premises of their lives. (Biggart, 1989,
> p. 97)

Those traditional premises accord status to spouses. When a
woman is being recruited, she is encouraged to talk the opportunity over with her husband. Some distributors ask a recruit
to bring the husband to hear the marketing plan so that his
questions can be answered. Distributors are encouraged to
obtain their husband's support for their Mary Kay activities
and to learn how to manage their business with minimal dis-
ruption to their husband's lives. Recruits are told that an advantage of Mary Kay is that "if your husband gets another
job, you can take the business with you" (October 25 Success
Meeting). Status within the Mary Kay organization does not
challenge the traditional family hierarchy.

In this section, I described the Mary Kay Inc. hierarchy. The company differentiates rank and generates multiple messages reconfirming status, while distributors validate status as success by aspiring to achieve these positions. Prosperity and status are combinatorial indicators of success as "consultants are on a journey to the top of the company ladder, moving up the company hierarchy by making money and acquiring material possessions, and their rank in the Company clearly is denoted through these material possessions" (Waggoner, 1994, p. 77).

A consultant becomes a red jacket by cultivating potential recruits, and her commissions increase. A director's stature grows as she nurtures more offspring directors and her commissions increase. A national sales director is responsible for having created a thriving branch of Mary Kay, and doing so ensures that her commissions increase. Women acclaim their status successes. But, their discourse is reframed to feminize the meaning of status and position their own status within the dominant hierarchy.

PERSONAL TRANSFORMATION AS SUCCESS

Cathy concludes the meeting by asking how many of the women present are glad they chose Mary Kay. All of the distributors raise their hands. Cathy suggests that Mary Kay is a better life for most women and the opportunity to receive recognition. Mary Kay is a self-improvement course. She asks them to share the Mary Kay opportunity with others this week. (September 27 Success Meeting)

June shows me some recruiting materials she has been putting together to use when she interviews potential Mary Kay consultants. She calls my attention to the opening statement. It reads, "Mary Kay is in the business of changing lives daily." (January 26 interview)

Through Mary Kay, a woman can be transformed into her better self. Success in this community of women can be achieved through personal growth. In this section, I describe growth in Mary Kay as involving particular forms of transformation and I argue that growth narratives are acceptable woman stories, but they are redefined and reconciled with traditionally masculine behaviors.

Transformation through Mary Kay

Transformation through personal growth pervades traditions and stories narrated by Cathy's Comets. The initiation ceremony compares women to blossoming rosebuds. The introduction of this chapter describes the ceremony in which a recruit is provided with a single rose and Cathy recites the formulaic liturgy: "Mary Kay says that when you join the company you're like a tiny rosebud and the longer you're in the company, the more you blossom and grow and become the woman God intended you to be." Growth is at the center of Mary Kay's philosophy of personal success.

> I like to remind directors of this truth when they ask me to autograph one-dollar bills as awards for their consultants. Next to my name I write, "Matthew 25: 14–30," which is the parable of the talents. It tells us to use and increase whatever God has given us, and that when we do, we shall be given more. I deeply believe in this philosophy, and I've always applied it throughout my business career. (Ash, 1984, p. 91)

God has "planted the seeds of greatness," and each woman can grow into her potential by taking the journey to an enriched self. A feature in *Applause* describes the flowering of a woman who advanced to the highest rank of national sales director.

> I questioned everything. I realize now that the journey was filled with all the necessary stepping-stones of self growth. Today I know I am truly ready for what lies ahead . . . I hope to help other women catch a glimpse of what they might be. I'm a good example of this company's way of building people from the inside out. ("NSD Debut," 1993, p. 27)

By virtue of her position, this woman is successful, but she has also achieved victory at a personal level, having undergone a transformation "from the inside out."

Personal growth in the Mary Kay community becomes a way of life. Specifically, growth occurs when a woman (1) believes she is in control of her own success, (2) overcomes her fears by stepping outside her comfort zone, (3) interprets obstacles and disappointments as learning experiences, and (4) develops a "go-give" attitude.

Assuming control of success. A woman grows when she believes she is capable of succeeding, establishing self-discipline, making decisions, and setting goals. June describes herself as unwilling to control the direction of her life prior to Mary Kay. Her growth occurs when she seriously commits to Mary Kay as her career path.

> *Q:* Well, so far what would you say has been your major accomplishment?
>
> *June:* Well I have to think about that. My major personal accomplishment you know's not something monetary. I have a direction now and I made a career choice, which is something I hadn't been willing to do up until this point. (October 26 interview)

Personal success is explicitly distinguished from monetary success in this account of her accomplishments. Like June, it is possible for Mary Kay consultants to earn success and recognition by personal growth even before they have acquired prosperity and status.

Overcoming fears. A woman grows when she overcomes her fears. Mary Kay distributors talk about their fears of speaking before others, interacting with strangers, and facing rejection. Amy recounts her ongoing struggle with her fears as she works toward growth in Mary Kay:

I'm trying to step out of my comfort zone a little bit more and present my card to people. I did yesterday at the copy shop. I was very proud of myself. . . . I sat down at this table with these two women. And I just kind of started and asked "so have you been waiting long?" In my heart of hearts, I just wanted to hand them both a card right then. But the fear thing was coming up for me. So then they called my name out and my stuff was done and so as I was standing there getting ready to pay and everything I thought the one lady had such pretty eyelashes and I thought I'm just going to ask her if she wants to model for me [i.e., attend a Mary Kay meeting for a makeover and recruiting presentation]. So I took my card over and she was just thrilled that I asked her, you know. (October 22 interview)

Amy consciously battles her fears and acclaims her own growth when she is able to step "outside her comfort zone" to enact the behaviors expected of Mary Kay distributors (e.g., talk Mary Kay to anyone who gets within three feet).

Sally, a red jacket, is farther along in her journey than Amy, but recounts her early fear experiences.

Cathy asks each of the red jackets to tell an audience that includes several potential recruits why she has chosen Mary Kay. Sally takes the microphone and begins to speak: "I'm Sally. I'm not afraid of this microphone anymore. Mary Kay is like the rose that opens up so that you can be what God intended you to be. Mary Kay has made me have a more positive personality. At the beginning, I was afraid and shook for weeks. I'm not afraid to stand up in front of others anymore. It has helped my personal growth. This is a support group. It is a group of sisters and family to me." (October 25 Success Meeting)

Sally overcomes her fear of speaking through her own determination and her association with women in the Mary Kay community.

Converting obstacles to opportunities.   A woman in this community develops when she realizes that obstacles and disappointments can be transformed into opportunities. Sarah almost won a car, but her team failed to earn $4000 in wholesale for four consecutive months.

> *Q:* What would you say has been your major accomplishment in Mary Kay so far?

> *Sarah:* Well I guess a major thing I would have to say would be the fact that I recruited—I brought into the company 10 people. . . . And that I—the fact that I did three months car production. I mean I missed it in the fourth month but you know I'm going again. But the fact that I could do it showed me that "Ok, I can do this." I've just got to work and do it. (October 12 interview)

The ability to turn "lemons into lemonade" and "snap back" from disappointment is a sign of growth. Persistence and commitment is recognized by others as contributing to future successes. June, one of Sarah's recruits, explains that Sarah and Tina, the most active red jackets in the group at this time, experienced difficulty completing car production, but they grew from having had the experience.

> I watched her [Tina] get so close to reaching her Grand Am and she's been through some really frustrating months but she's turned it around into a positive, a positive self-growth. Look at Sarah. You know I think Sarah and Tina will be better directors because they've had that experience. (October 26 interview)

The stories told by the women experiencing disappointment and the stories told about these women affirm the salience of challenges as an important part of the growth process.

Embracing the go-give principle. A Mary Kay woman grows as she becomes the embodiment of the "go-give" principle, Mary Kay's adaptation of the golden rule. A woman with go-give spirit is positive, enthusiastic, cooperative, helpful, and connected to others. She learns to turn her life around. Elizabeth's story tells how Mary Kay helped her to turn her life

around. She explains the kind of person she was when Cathy
approached her about Mary Kay:

> Cathy approached me one day at church and she com-
> plimented me. This is the funny thing. At that particular time
> when she complimented me, I kind of had the attitude, "Oh
> right." That's why I say if it hadn't been for Cathy I don't
> know where I'd be right now. I was always the type of
> person who was a little suspicious of people and what they
> would say to you. I kind of had a chip on my shoulder and
> a little bit of anger in my heart over my past life and things
> like this. And I just didn't trust people. (November 1 interview)

Now, Elizabeth exudes the go-give attitude as she recounts
how her experience in Mary Kay changed her personality:

> I'm Elizabeth. I've been in Mary Kay for three years. What
> is the most important thing? I think it's building other women's
> self-esteem. It is being able to make other women glow. It is
> the friendship. It has transformed me. I was a hard case to
> convince. I have a softer heart now. I enjoy being with the
> people. It's all because of Cathy. I was a tough cookie and
> I changed. Ladies, look into it. (December 13 Success Meeting)

Elizabeth's previous self was distrustful while her new self—
developed as a Mary Kay consultant—is compassionate.

The value assigned to this particular display of personal
growth is demonstrated by the prestige accorded to the Miss
Go-Give award, presented annually to the woman who best
exemplifies this principle. Bev distinguishes it from awards for
economic success:

> And the highest award in the company is the Go-Give award.
> I mean it's not for sales accomplishment. It's for helping your
> neighbor. (November 2 interview)

Recipients of the award are proud of it. When I asked Sarah
to describe the many Mary Kay pins that covered the lapel of
her red jacket, she began by pointing to the Miss Go-Give pin
and characterized it as her "most prized."

The growth expected in Mary Kay pervades a woman's personality and becomes a way of life. Lois, a consultant for only seven months, describes an awareness of her transformation as she attended Success Meetings.

> At first, it was either you're kind of embarrassed because everybody, I mean, it's I guess it comes back to the comfort zone. You're not used to being that type of person, and uh, now I feel like since I have started being that person I'm that person all the time, more, more of the time, you know. I get more excited about things than I used to, I used to hide it, I guess. But now I, just, not only in Mary Kay, in my other life and job also. (November 15 interview)

This new self is nurtured in Success Meetings and begins to emerge at other times and places as this identity becomes a way of life.

An assumption implicit in the growth metaphor is that women need to grow, although their specific needs and the amount of growth necessary to be successful may vary. For example, June had always been an extrovert and had no fear of strangers but needed to take control of her own success. Cathy explains that differences in the timing of success (defined here as status and prosperity) are attributable to differences in personal growth:

> I know there are people in this company that become Directors in six months. There are people it takes 10 years. See I believe truly that we all have a different amount of growing to do and whenever you have to grow into that position, you know? Does that make sense, you know? There's people who come in and they've already been in other careers and jobs that they're ready to do that quicker and to learn and they know how to manage people. (December 7 interview)

This belief intersects with meritocracy, any woman can be successful in Mary Kay. Distributors who experience delay in reaching economic or status goals in Mary Kay simply need further time before they "grow into the position" where prosperity is assured. A woman's personal growth precedes increasing economic and status rewards. Each woman will vary in the amount of growth necessary, but every woman requires some growth. A woman who rejects or fails to complete a personal conversion will not be as successful in Mary Kay. Waggoner (1994) describes the Mary Kay experience as a journey to the ideal, that women seek to be the same ideal character. The negative implication is the loss of a sense of self but a positive outcome may be obtained in the collaborative effort to create a single identity.

Redefining the success story about personal growth. To construe success as personal growth is consistent with a cultural ideology that feminizes personal development. Hardesty and Jacobs (1986) argue a woman has an "inherently female yearning for self-improvement" so that her satisfaction is assessed by "how much she grows from and is enriched by the experience" (pp. 34–35). In contrast, men derive their satisfaction from promotions, advancements, and the acquisition of wealth (Hardesty & Jacobs, 1986; Hennig & Jardim, 1977). When Mary Kay women tell their stories of personal transformation, they are telling a woman story in a form that is recognizable and acceptable within our culture.

The recasting of this definition of success is displayed in the forms of personal growth expected in Mary Kay. Women are encouraged to change their ways of thinking and adopt behaviors typically associated with a masculine role while continuing to maintain their femininity. Traits and behaviors consistent with the instrumental male gender role are being "competent, independent, objective, active, competitive, logical, able to make decisions easily, self-confident, dominant, and desiring prestigious careers for their own needs" (Steinberg, 1984, pp. 3–4). Women's expressive roles include "gentleness, kindness, warmth, sensitivity, emotionality, passivity, dependence, tactfulness, noncompetitiveness, and desiring positions where they can help others" (Steinberg, 1984, p. 4).

A woman grows in Mary Kay when she takes control of her own success, declaring competence and independence. She grows when she overcomes her fears and becomes assertive and active. A woman grows when she embraces obstacles as opportunities, which strengthens her confidence. The types of growth that would lead to these behaviors are more commonly associated with the male instrumental role than the female expressive role. A Mary Kay woman can do all this and remain gentle, warm, noncompetitive, and helpful to others.

It is possible for Mary Kay women to tell their transformation stories. These narratives employ a woman story form, and they are told in the context of the most important form of growth, learning to live life by the go-give principle. Mary Kay women believe that "go-givers are go-getters," that success is more likely when an individual is positive, enthusiastic, cooperative, helpful, and connected to others. The go-give principle firmly roots women's growth in their femininity and creates a growth narrative that reconciles the addition of traditionally masculine behaviors.

In summary, personal growth is another meaning for success in this Mary Kay community. Prosperity and status are dependent upon having achieved this form of success. Women grow in Mary Kay by assuming control of success, overcoming fears, converting obstacles to opportunities, and embracing the go-give principle. A transformational narrative is an acceptable woman story. But these stories are redefined by their inclusion of forms of growth that have been traditionally part of the masculine gender role. The story is tellable because of the familiar form and the relative importance of the go-give attitude, which coincides with the feminine gender role.

CONCLUSION

Multiple meanings of success are constructed within the Mary Kay community. Prosperity as success is promoted by the company and embraced by distributors in Cathy's Comets. This form of success endorses the capitalistic drive to make money and is consistent with an enduring definition of American success as wealth (Biggart, 1983; Cawelti, 1965; Chenoweth, 1974; Huber, 1971; Wyllie, 1954). But the success stories told by Mary Kay women are redefined as acts of caring and the affirmation of the priority of family. Status as a definition of success sanctions an elaborate organizational hierarchy. The company designates rank, and distributors validate this form of success by aspiring to achieve respected positions. The success stories about status are redefined by feminizing status and defining status within the dominant hierarchy. Success can also be achieved through personal growth. Transformation stories are understandable woman stories, albeit the forms of growth include masculine behaviors and traits. These redefinitions of growth expand the meaning of personal transformation while maintaining intelligibility through a familiar form and the importance of a feminine "go-give" attitude.

The desire for success is pervasive in our culture. This chapter has described how women in Mary Kay affirm the meaning of success and come to redefine their success stories to make them understandable and acceptable within the culture. This understanding provides the necessary grounding for examining the acclaiming and disclaiming in the success discourse of Mary Kay distributors in the next chapter.

5

How the Dream is Realized

*Talking about Success in
Mary Kay Cosmetics*

*If someone else will just believe in
you—you will be able to do great
things. I know this because someone
believed in me. At a time when I may
not have displayed much in the way of
experience or skill—someone believed
that I could succeed. And largely because of this confidence, I did!*
—Mary Kay Ash on success

*There is absolutely no reason why a
woman should not succeed in business.
All she needs is: Intuitiveness; Foresight; Product knowledge; Market
knowledge; Guts; Lipstick; Clear judgment; A stubborn streak; A computer.*
—Mary Kay Ash on success

In her autobiography, Mary Kay Ash shares her experience
and advice on success. As the charismatic founder of a business
producing $613 million in sales (Farnham, 1993), she has much
to convey about how a woman's dream to succeed can be
realized. Talk about success is ubiquitous in the Mary Kay
culture. Distributors tell success stories about how they are
accomplishing their dreams through Mary Kay Cosmetics. While
chapter 4 described the meaning of "success" in Mary Kay
Inc., this chapter details the discursive strategies of the success
stories of distributors in a Mary Kay unit. Following a brief
excursion into method, the analysis is organized by acclaiming

(entitlements and enhancements) and disclaiming (dissociations and detractions) discourse.

METHOD

This analysis is based on observations of Cathy's Comets weekly Mary Kay Success Meetings over a period of five months, interviews of 13 Mary Kay distributors, and materials produced by the national office and the director (e.g., newsletters, magazines, audiotapes, advertisements, books). These materials were reviewed for personal success stories (i.e., those stories told about the teller's own successes). The constant comparison method described in previous chapters was applied to the success stories to generate and refine a framework of discursive strategies for explaining that success (Glaser & Strauss, 1967; Strauss, 1990). Stories were examined for strategies relevant to the goals of securing recognition and appearing modest. An initial typology of strategies was refined, theoretical memoing procedures moved descriptions to abstract levels, and the analysis was sharpened to create a meaningful fit. ETHNOGRAPH, a computer program for sorting ethnographic data, was useful for coding the discourse and refining the analysis. Negative instances were used to modify the analysis (Jacobs, 1988). The appendix provides additional methodological details.

ANALYSIS

The analysis is subdivided into a description of discourse designed to acclaim a success to secure recognition and of discourse that attends to disclaiming a success to appear modest. Table 5.1 provides a summary of the acclaiming and disclaiming strategies used by Mary Kay distributors in their success stories.

TABLE 5.1

A Typology of Strategies for Acclaiming and Disclaiming Discourse in Mary Kay Success Stories

Acclaiming

Entitlement Strategies

1. Tellers recount that they worked hard to earn their success.
2. Tellers report that they persevered in their work.
3. Tellers show they are willing to take risks.
4. Tellers demonstrate that they accomplished their success independently.

Enhancement Strategies

1. Tellers demonstrate that their success realized a higher purpose.
2. Tellers indicate their success is acquired rapidly.
3. Tellers recount that their success is acquired efficiently.
4. Tellers show how their success is recognized and rewarded by others.
5. Tellers describe their success as fulfilling a dream.
6. Tellers indicate their success required overcoming obstacles.

Disclaiming

Dissociation Strategies

1. Tellers share responsibility for their success.
2. Tellers attribute their success to external or uncontrollable causes.
3. Tellers express surprise at their unexpected success or recognition.

Detraction Strategies

1. Tellers note their success is less noteworthy compared to other accomplishments.
2. Tellers suggest their success is incomplete.

ACCLAIMING DISCOURSE

Acclaiming discourse persuades the audience of success stories that the teller is responsible for a success and that the success is worthy of recognition. Entitlement and enhancement strategies enact a teller's attempts to shape an audience's perceptions of a desirable event. Mary Kay distributors are keen to convince their audience of other Mary Kay members that they are achieving economic, status, and personal success.

Entitlement Strategies

An accomplishment becomes an individual's success when the person telling the story can demonstrate that she is responsible for that success (D'Arcy, 1963). Tellers assert responsibility for a success by recounting that they (1) worked hard to earn their success, (2) persevered in their work, (3) are willing to take risks to be successful, and (4) accomplished the success independently. These discursive strategies imply that tellers possess personal characteristics that account for their own successes.

Tellers recount that they worked hard to earn their success. Cathy's January newsletter sent to all of her distributors proclaims; "Success is no fable—just hard work" (January newsletter, p. 4). The message is consistent with Mary Kay Ash's belief that "neither desire or knowledge is enough [for success]. The third requirement is that you apply yourself" (Ash, 1987, p. 120). In the Mary Kay culture, individual effort is the antecedent to success. Personal success stories demonstrate how Mary Kay distributors have worked hard for their achievements.

Effort is an internal cause for success, so credit is attributed to the individual who exerted that effort. Mary Kay distributors display that they work hard by telling others what they are doing to increase their business.

> Trish shows June her calendar for the month. Mary Kay classes are marked prominently in pink ink. There are at least three classes booked each week and several days include two bookings for the same day. June offers enthusiastic praise and tells Trish she is doing great! She spends several minutes looking at the calendar while Trish smiles. (January 24 Success Meeting)

Trish provides evidence of working hard by directing attention to her schedule of upcoming classes. These classes are opportunities to sell the product and to recruit. Setting these classes up required individual initiative and multiple phone calls. Trish is demonstrating to June that she is doing what is expected of a successful Mary Kay distributor, and June's response confirms that this effort is worthy of recognition.

Fran accounts for her fast start in Mary Kay by describing the work she does each week:

> I try to spend three evenings a week and that includes Monday nights. Because I've not—since I've become a consultant I have not missed a Monday night 5:30 facial and nail class. . . . I've always had a guest and so I include that as one work evening and then in addition to that I schedule two other either facial or nail care classes or something. . . . Now that doesn't include one night in addition to that I spend making phone calls either for reorders or scheduling classes for the next week and then I spend another evening a week writing out my weekly report, putting product on the shelf, ordering product. (November 11 interview)

She recounts in great detail how many evenings she spends working her business. Her telling of the kind of work communicates that she is doing what is necessary to succeed according to Mary Kay—attending the weekly meetings, scheduling classes, devoting much of her free time to her business. She is working at success.

Mary Kay distributors earn star consultant honors when they attain lofty monthly sales or recruiting goals. Becky explains that her success in becoming a star consultant occurs because she was willing to work.

> This [ruby star consultant ring] was one particular ring I really wanted so I really worked for it. (November 8 interview)

The ring is a motivator for the effort that leads to economic and status success. In recounting how she earned the star consultant honors, she explains that her success is the result of her hard work.

Tellers report that they persevered in their work. Perseverance implies that persistence and patient effort are individual qualities. Thus, responsibility for a success caused by perseverance can be attributed to the teller. In acclaiming her success, Cathy, the director, focuses on her perseverance as a primary reason her unit was able to make $400,000 in sales the first year.

> Part of it's perseverance. Just not giving up. I guess I'm a person, you know, when I commit myself to something, I guess I stay in there and keep working at it until—I'm not a person who gives up very easily. I might have been shy and quiet, but I was also determined. And I think determination and perseverance and just not ever giving up and knowing that if you keep doing it, that finally you'll figure out how to do it right. (December 7 interview)

Cathy suggests that perseverance and dedication are enduring personality traits. As such, they become attributes for which she can assert responsibility in acclaiming her success.

Tina was viewed by other distributors as one of the most successful Mary Kay distributors in Cathy's Comets. She was a team manager and on target for her car. In her personal success story, she explains that perseverance is essential to her accomplishments:

> I think it [one of the qualities leading to my success] is not giving up. I got discouraged. Because I did several interviews and nobody said yes . . . I just kept at it and I kept believing in the company. And I think that's what I'm learning. You can't give up. (October 21 interview)

The prominence of "I" in Tina's explanation is further evidence that perseverance is being characterized as an individual attribute. Because persistence can be learned and controlled, a distributor increases responsibility for a success by explaining that it is the result of persistence.

Tellers show they are willing to take risks. Mary Kay distributors can achieve the highest levels of success by committing themselves to Mary Kay Inc. as their only occupation. Most distributors begin by selling Mary Kay part time while holding other jobs but aspire to selling Mary Kay on a full-time basis. Distributors assume financial risks when they decide to quit traditional jobs and work their Mary Kay business full time. They forego an assured income and fringe benefits. The outcome is uncertain, but there is the potential for great success. Simone recently made this decision and shared her account of the challenge:

> It was very scary [to do Mary Kay full time]. It was very scary. . . . I'm a very security-oriented person and I was, like, I probably about had a mental breakdown because it was such a challenge to think about doing something that I didn't know if I could do. (October 5 interview)

The uncertainty poses a financial and personal risk and yet Simone commits herself to Mary Kay and is successful in meeting the challenge.

A sales director's success story is featured prominently in a Mary Kay recruiting brochure. The story directly connects her willingness to assume the financial risk of doing Mary Kay full time with her rapid success.

> After more than a year of learning the business, loving the success and working through the tough times, Caren with Seth's encouragement, moved out "on faith." She quit her full time job in November. . . . In July she became a team manager and on December 1 Caren debuted as a Sales Director. ("Discover for Yourself," 1992, p. 3)

She achieves success quickly when she is willing to endanger her own financial security "on faith." The willingness to take calculated risks in order to succeed increases a distributor's responsibility for the resulting success.

Tellers demonstrate that they accomplished their success independently. This discursive strategy amplifies responsibility for the success by maintaining that the distributor achieves it without the direct assistance of others. A Mary Kay distributor claims that she owns her own business and her accomplishments are to her credit.

Tina reflects that when she earned her red jacket, an important status success in Mary Kay, she deserved the credit for the accomplishment:

> And I thought, "Gosh, I did this myself." That's been a factor. I haven't always thought I've done things alone. There's always been someone there to help. (October 21 interview)

In contrast to prior experiences, Tina values Mary Kay because the company allows her to establish an independent distributorship and she can accomplish the success without feeling dependent on others. She asserts responsibility for her own success at the same time she argues that she is in control of her own destiny.

The four strategies in this section are directed toward convincing an audience that the distributor should be given credit for her Mary Kay achievements. Taking credit (Decker, 1987; Giacalone, 1985) is considerably elaborated in Mary Kay success stories. Of the three case studies analyzed in this book, Mary Kay distributors have the most fully developed set of entitlement strategies.

Women, as tellers of success stories, face a particularly difficult task. Women's successes are perceived as unexpected and attributed to external causes by both male and female audiences (Deaux & Emswiller, 1974; Etaugh & Brown, 1975; Giacalone & Riordan, 1990). As Mary Kay distributors tell their success stories about economic, status, and personal success, they must convince their audience they are actually responsible for their success. But, as I argued in chapter 4, their stories must remain intelligible to be heard. Stories about making money and earning status are not traditional woman stories.

The successes of men are attributed to ability while the successes of women are explained as the result of luck or effort (Deaux & Emswiller, 1974; Etaugh & Brown, 1975; Giacalone & Riordan, 1990). The first entitlement strategy of demonstrating how hard a distributor worked to earn success attributes an internal but unstable attribution. Perseverance can also be viewed as an indication of effort. Success achieved as a result of effort rather than ability receives less recognition (Giacalone & Riordan, 1990; Heilman & Guzzo, 1978). In using these first two entitlement strategies, Mary Kay distributors are confirming expectations about women's successes. When they do occur, they can be explained by effort rather than ability.

Gender expectations are reflected in clusters of traits distinguishing women from men (Broverman, Vogel, Broverman, Clarkson, & Rosenkrantz, 1972; Deaux, 1976; Innes, Dormer, & Lukins, 1993; Six & Eckes, 1991). A cluster of traits reflecting warmth and expressiveness are associated with women. They are typically seen as gentle, able to express their feelings, empathic, and tactful. A cluster of traits exhibiting competence are associated with men. Men are viewed as dominant, competitive, independent, active, and ambitious. The last two entitlement strategies that connect responsibility for a success with a willingness to take risks and achieve success independently are assertions of traditionally masculine traits. These strategies are unique to this case study and acclaim a success by challenging gender expectations.

Mary Kay distributors display a more developed set of entitlement strategies than the other case studies examined. They face the additional complication of telling a *woman's* success story. The entitlement strategies unique to this case study challenge gender expectations about success to acclaim Mary Kay successes.

Enhancement Strategies

Individuals can also acclaim their own successes by magnifying the importance of the achievement. Telling a success story generates more recognition if the success itself is noteworthy. Like the athletes described in chapter 3, Mary Kay distributors display an extensive repertoire of strategies for highlighting the significance of their successes. Cultural expectations that women's successes are both unexpected and less worthy of recognition place Mary Kay distributors in the position of persuading their audience that selling cosmetics is, in fact, a significant success. Tellers of these success stories magnify their success by demonstrating that it (1) realized a higher purpose, (2) is acquired rapidly, (3) is acquired efficiently, (4) is recognized and rewarded by others, (5) realized a dream, and (6) required overcoming obstacles.

Tellers demonstrate that their success realized a higher purpose. This enhancement strategy increases the significance of a success by associating it with a noble goal. To succeed in Mary Kay is also to serve God, to facilitate the success of other Mary Kay distributors, to teach and enrich customer's lives, and to nurture one's own family. Success is redefined as an act of spirituality and giving, serving a much higher purpose than an individual's acquisition of wealth through cosmetic sales.

"I truly believe the growth of Mary Kay Cosmetics has come about because the first thing we did was to take God as our partner," Mary Kay Ash reveals in her autobiography (Ash, 1987, p. 62). Her company was blessed by God and as a result "miracles have happened with women growing to become all God knew He had created" ("30 Years of Dreams," 1993, p. 6). As women succeed in Mary Kay, they reaffirm God's faith and wisdom.

Cathy, the director of the unit, explains that her success was made possible once she understood that she could do God's work through Mary Kay. When she felt frustrated, she asked God for a sign:

> I just said, "God somehow let me know if this is what you want me to do." . . . I felt like I was making a difference in other people's lives. . . . In my heart I really felt God needed me to know why I was doing this, you know? And so I became a director then. (December 7 interview)

The sign came when a new recruit signed up to be a Mary Kay consultant and this gave Cathy enough unit members to form her own unit. Her success is important because it is a means to achieve God's work by making a difference in her distributors' lives.

Success is enhanced when the altruistic purpose of helping other women achieve their "God-given potential" is emphasized. Mary Kay distributors can achieve this purpose by sharing the Mary Kay opportunity and then assisting their recruits to success. A national sales director aligns this noble purpose with the Mary Kay philosophy:

> I'm caught up in the whole Mary Kay philosophy, the whole Mary Kay spirit. My dream now is for each one of my Directors to become better than I ever was. (Ash, 1987, pp. 189–190)

The competitive drive for individual success is eclipsed by a sincere desire to help others succeed. At the unit level, Tina explains that her own success comes from caring about the success of her team:

> So maybe there might be something about me in the way I care about people and want them to succeed as well. I think that's the other thing. Getting the "me" out of it and that we work together. (October 21 interview)

Her success is particularly significant because it is motivated by aspirations for other women in Mary Kay.

A higher purpose can also be served by selling Mary Kay Cosmetics to customers. By teaching women to make the most of their physical appearance through the use of cosmetics, distributors achieve a higher purpose by enhancing the self-esteem of their customers.

> But so much of it, so much of the company's emphasis, is not really on selling, but having the other person feel better about themselves and just providing a service. (November 2 interview with Bev)

> Skin care classes become opportunities to reach out and touch another life. (January newsletter, p. 3)

Distributors see their business as helping their customers "feel better about themselves." Their successes (particularly economic successes) are reframed and achieve significance by virtue of their noble purpose.

A Mary Kay success can be enhanced by making it possible to achieve the higher purpose of caring for family (also see chapter 4). In Mary Kay Inc., women can nurture their families by working fewer hours than a traditional job would require, yet still assisting their family financially.

> I also love the fact that I can financially contribute to my family and still pick up my kids at school! ("Dare to Dream," 1993, p. 7)

By helping family members, a success achieves a higher purpose than individual gain. The success is worthy of recognition.

Serving God, customers, recruits, and family—rather than self—enhances the importance of the success. Success obtained through Mary Kay is redefined, made intelligible, and granted significance by achieving a higher purpose.

Tellers indicate their success is acquired rapidly. A woman who becomes successful early in her Mary Kay career or acquires the next position on the Mary Kay hierarchy quickly can point to her record as evidence of the magnitude of her success. Not only has she accomplished a feat that is remarkable in itself, but she has done it in record time. Her history becomes part of her "I" story, to be told and retold to other distributors. Her meteoric rise makes her success distinctive, and extraordinary abilities are implied. The director of Cathy's Comets shares a story she told often to her consultants about her ascension in the Mary Kay hierarchy:

> We went to Seminar that year and I mean when we debuted as a unit, you had to debut with 24 people and a year later in December we had 96 people. So we really built fast! . . . I mean, we won a pink car the fastest you could win one after as a unit. And then that year we did $400,000. That's really great for your first year. (December 7 interview)

Cathy's success story emphasizes the acquisition of status and material symbols of directorship, the number of consultants, and a pink car, while highlighting that these "great" successes were acquired rapidly.

In another example, the swift route to success figures prominently in the success narrative.

> I had five recruits because I had gone on target for my car. It was like the first five recruits came very steady. Like within a month. (October 21 interview with Tina)

Tina draws attention to the short time that elapsed between being a consultant and a team manager (with a minimum of five recruits and the opportunity to earn a Mary Kay car). To have progressed at this rate in only a month enhances the achievement.

The prior examples illustrate that status successes are acclaimed. But economic successes are also evaluated more positively when they occur swiftly.

> I did something like $15,000 in sales my first and second years in Mary Kay. (November 1 interview with Elizabeth)

Elizabeth recounts sales totals earning top sales honors for the unit and links this achievement with her early years in Mary Kay. The remarkable sales figures are made more praiseworthy by the fact that they occurred quickly.

Tellers recount that they acquired the success efficiently. Mary Kay women learn to make "smart money" by investing their limited time in activities that pay large dividends (September 20 Success Meeting). Their choices stand in contrast to corporate women, who work long hours and sacrifice their relationships with family to earn comparable incomes. In the ritual for identifying the winner of top sales honors, Cathy routinely asks and consultants volunteer information regarding the number of hours worked as part of their success narratives.

> Sarah says she worked three hours and earned $75 an hour. The audience applauds enthusiastically. (October 4 Success Meeting)

> Barb reports that she earned $55.96 per hour on sales of $940. The audience applauds. (November 22 Success Meeting)

Successful distributors tell other consultants that they earn good money with a minimal time investment.

Distributors also earn "smart money" by establishing a customer base to generate a reorder business.

> I never even left my home and made $150 this week in net profit [through reorders]. (November 1 interview with Elizabeth)

> Lois says she has been in Mary Kay for seven months and gets more reorders all the time and that this lets her make more profit per hour. (October 4 Success Meeting)

Whether it is by working a few hours at a class, building a reorder business, recruiting others, or offering incentives for hostesses to sell additional product (September 20 Success Meeting), these stories of individual success display the efficiency with which Mary Kay distributors earn money. Their proficiency in achieving success enhances the value of that success.

Tellers show how their success is recognized and rewarded by others. Successes meriting distinction are rewarded by meaningful symbols in public rituals when Mary Kay distributors meet as a group. At Seminar, the national meeting of Mary Kay distributors, the symbols of success are the ultimate Cinderella gifts: cars, furs, and diamonds. The rituals of appearing on stage with Mary Kay and identifying the Queen's Courts are considered ultimate successes. The Mary Kay culture is replete with awards and award rituals.

In describing her success in a newsletter, Catherine recounts her selection in the Queen's Court of Sales at Seminar:

> Going across stage feels so glamorous and so GRAND. It is
> a special highlight that I don't think I'll ever forget. (August-
> TX newsletter, p. 1)

The significance of her recognition in this particular ritual
is acclaimed with strong evaluative language defining its
importance.

At the weekly Success Meetings of Cathy's Comets, there
are rituals proclaiming success for the go-give attitude, high
sales, basic set sales, weekly challenges, bar pins for cumulative
sales since the last Seminar, and the pinning of new consultants. Mary Kay consultants win pearls, diamond rings, bumblebee pins (symbolizing success against all odds), ribbons, and
lunches with the director, among numerous other honors. The
audience signifies its approval through applause. The culture
determines the nature of success and the recognitions for
achievements. Distributors depict economic, status, and personal successes as worthy of praise because they are recognized
and rewarded by the culture. For example, when Tina describes her accomplishments, she points to the high sales rituals and the rewards she has received in Mary Kay:

> I love it when Cathy asks who worked their business and I
> can stand up and say I had greater than a $300 week. Or
> being able to get the pearls. I mean my necklace is almost
> full of pearls and spacers. Star consultant. Because that says
> to people "wow." You're working your business consistently
> and never did I dream I would be a diamond star consultant
> last time. But it just worked out that way. (October 21
> interview)

Tina begins by appreciating the importance of the ritual Cathy
uses at every Success Meeting for identifying the distributor
with the highest weekly sales. She indicates that she can exceed
the goal of $300 a week that is an established part of the
3+3+3 plan for success (have $300 a week in sales, give the
marketing plan to three people, and hold three classes). The
pearls and spacers are given for the sales of basic sets and Tina
acclaims her success by reporting that her necklace is nearly

complete. Star consultants must attain a high level of sales for the quarter and Tina enhances her economic success by indicating that she was recently a diamond star consultant (i.e., the highest level recognized by Mary Kay, requiring $3000 in sales for the quarter). Tina enhances her success by pointing out that they are recognized as important within the Mary Kay culture.

Economic successes are awarded by bar pins, pearls for basic sets, Queen of Sales honors; status successes are awarded by distinctive clothing and pins, cars, trips; personal successes are awarded by Miss Go-Give honors and praise. In describing any of these forms of recognition in a success story, distributors indicate they have earned the approval of their social group. The recognition is important because it signifies success within the Mary Kay culture.

Tellers describe their success as fulfilling a dream. Dreams represent aspirations. A success characterized as the realization of a dream is marked as a special accomplishment. In this first example, Rose tells the story about being in the Queen's Court of Sales at Seminar:

> Coming down those stairs, going across stage, getting my diamond ring, it all seemed like a dream. And it is. A dream come true. (August-TX newsletter, p. 1)

The dream is to accomplish the pinnacle of success in sales in Mary Kay, to be named to the Queen's Court of Sales. Rose's recounting of this milestone as the realization of her dream enhances its importance.

Similarly, Cathy tells consultants about her successes in earning top directors' trips:

> How many of you have gone on a trip to Australia, Greece, Canada, all expenses paid for yourself and your husband because you did a great job at work? Well David and I have been to all those places with Mary Kay. And they are wonderful trips. Dreams really can come true. (October 25 Success Meeting)

Her words connect her own successes to the realization of a dream that has been achieved through Mary Kay. Success in Mary Kay makes it possible to achieve dreams in which women are recognized and pampered.

Tellers indicate their success required overcoming obstacles. This strategy magnifies the importance of the success by describing it as difficult and demanding. Accomplishments that require a struggle are valued more highly than easy successes. Cathy proclaims in her January newsletter:

> The mark of a person is not how far and fast he runs from his problems, but how well he meets, faces, and deals with those problems. That is truly the mark of a Great Human Being. (January newsletter, p. 4)

A success becomes even more remarkable when obstacles are surmounted.

Sue, one of Cathy's offspring directors, explains that one of her obstacles was learning to be more in control of her success by setting goals:

> Well before Mary Kay I didn't even have goals. I just took whatever came and figured that was what I was supposed to have. (November 3 interview)

Through Mary Kay, Sue learned to set specific goals and advanced to the position of a director. Sue's current goal includes becoming a Cadillac director (i.e., the unit sells $100,000 wholesale in two quarters). A personal obstacle is overcome, and her potential for success is limitless when she realizes that she controls her goals.

Fears are a prominent obstacle for Mary Kay distributors. Cathy tells her disbelieving unit that she was once shy and fearful of speaking in front of a group of other women. Some distributors fear engaging strangers in "warm chatter." Others fear rejection when they approach other women about hosting classes and recruiting. Kelly has demonstrated her recruiting success by earning her red jacket. In telling her success story,

she shows that she used to fear rejection but overcame it to
share the Mary Kay opportunity with others.

> When Cathy asked Kelly to explain how she became a red
> jacket, Kelly says she was initially scared to ask people if
> they were interested in the Mary Kay opportunity. She was
> afraid of rejection. But she overcame that fear by approach-
> ing people and saying to them what the company advises a
> consultant to say as she is recruiting a new consultant. Kelly
> says she shouldn't have waited so long! That it was actually
> easy when she started to use what the company told her to
> say. (November 15 Success Meeting)

In overcoming her fears, she is able to recruit and move up the
Mary Kay hierarchy. An important obstacle has been conquered.

When Mary Kay distributors set high goals, they are not
always successful in their first attempts. But Mary Kay teaches
that a person "fails forward to success" (Ash, 1987, ch. 11) by
learning from mistakes. Sarah recounts how she learned from
her failures:

> I guess losing my red jacket and not getting my car in the
> fourth month and the way you overcome it is to continue to
> do it and not quitting. (October 12 interview)

These disappointments must be turned into learning experiences. Sarah magnifies the importance of her recent success in
earning back her red jacket by indicating that she has moved
past these obstacles.

Obstacles can take the form of negative thinking. This is
contrary to the go-give spirit associated with success in Mary
Kay. Amy shares that her skepticism has been a personal obstacle she has learned to overcome:

> It's taken—I'm such an incredible skeptic sometimes that it's
> taken me a long time to believe the things that other people
> tell me. So Mary Kay has helped me a little bit with a more
> positive attitude too. (October 22 interview)

Achieving a positive attitude is a form of personal transformation. There is every expectation that other forms of success will follow because go-givers are go-getters.

While the prior description details internal obstacles, Mary Kay distributors also tell stories about overcoming external impediments created by other people or the environment. Mary Kay distributors magnify the importance of their success by telling how they handled other jobs and family responsibilities, difficult customers, financial problems, illnesses, and a lack of support from others.

A visiting Mary Kay director told the consultants of Cathy's Comets how her bank job interfered with attendance at the Mary Kay Seminar.

> I told my boss . . . that I needed to have the week off for the Mary Kay Seminar. He told me to put in for it for my vacation. I had, but I got bumped off by other people. He told me to try to trade with someone. I tried and no one would trade. He told me to tell someone that my marriage was in trouble and I needed to have that time off to work on my marriage. I said I wouldn't lie. He said he could take it up with the board. He did and said they decided not to make an exception for me. On Monday morning, I turned in my letter of resignation. (October 11 Success Meeting)

She enumerates avenues she pursued, but her other job continued to create obstacles and her final resolution was to resign from her position at the bank. She decides to remove the other job as an obstacle.

Families can present an obstacle to success in Mary Kay because it is a challenge to balance the responsibilities and problems of raising a family with Mary Kay responsibilities. Becky has to deal with family pressures that make it difficult for her to sustain a positive attitude:

> I had too many pressures going on. . . . We've just had a lot from our family life with children that basically just caught up with us and caused our lives to not go as good as we want but we're really working on it. (November 8 interview)

She works to help herself and her family overcome these obstacles, and her Mary Kay business flourishes.

Customers pose obstacles when they cancel classes or are uncooperative. Kim describes a particularly obstinate customer that she managed to win over.

> Kim describes a big skin care class she had on Sunday. One of her customers was not too excited about being there. She was stand-offish and gave her a long list of what she wouldn't do before they even started. She wouldn't take off her makeup etc. . . . Kim recounts how she talked to her and melted her resistance. The client bought a hundred dollars of product. (November 15 Success Meeting)

Distributors learn to deal with different kinds of people and Kim's ability to overcome the customer's reluctance results in a large sale.

An illness can pose a severe obstacle to a distributor's Mary Kay career. Women who tell stories about their own illnesses show how they successfully met the challenge and refused to let it interrupt their commitment to Mary Kay.

> I had cancer last fall. . . . I knew that being in Mary Kay Cosmetics would help me get through all of it. And it's like I had my surgery on a Wednesday and I never missed a meeting. (November 2 interview with Bev)

Despite major surgery, Bev is present at the next Mary Kay Success Meeting. Her success story tells how she refused to allow the illness to pose an insurmountable obstacle to her life and her Mary Kay career.

Lack of support from others can be another hurdle on the road to success. Critical attitudes can be discouraging. Because most people want others to like them and respect their choices, it can be obstructive when these attitudes are held by significant others. Becky describes how she learned to discount these attitudes:

> "Oh like so you're selling makeup?" Things like that and "You're going to get a pink Cadillac?" And they'd make fun

of it. And I'd say, "Yes, I will eventually." I used to kind of get frustrated when they'd say it but now I say, "Yes, Yes I will, Yes I will," you know? "Oh are you sure?" And I'll say, "Yeah." Cause you might as well be as positive as you can about it. (November 8 interview)

Although Becky is bothered by the doubts, she tells about learning to maintain her own positive attitude. She refuses to allow other's negative attitudes to create barriers to her own success.

Enhancement strategies magnify the importance of a success. Of these six discursive strategies found in Mary Kay success discourse, only the description of obstacles have been previously discussed in the literature (Giacalone & Riordan, 1990). Enhancement strategies are prominent in the success stories of Mary Kay distributors because they counter dismissive cultural expectations regarding women's successes. These stories demonstrate that women are quite capable of earning economic, status, and personal success and that their successes are especially worthy of recognition. Mary Kay distributors, in particular, encounter individuals who deride the selling of cosmetics as a serious career choice and devalue the importance of a success in this enterprise. Even when Mary Kay distributors are addressing their success stories to other distributors, they must resist the devaluation of their efforts.

Like the athletes' strategies described in chapter 3, Mary Kay distributors enhance their successes by showing how they realize a dream and overcome obstacles. Like Nobel winners, their successes were able to realize a higher purpose and to overcome obstacles. The grounds for enhancing a success are used by predominantly men in the success stories in the prior cases. By claiming that their successes can be assessed by the same standards, they are implicitly making the argument that their success is worthy of recognition.

Three additional enhancement strategies are unique to Mary Kay distributors. First, tellers of success stories indicate that their successes are recognized and rewarded by others. What is implied in Nobel discourse is explicit in Mary Kay discourse. The badges of honor are worn more openly and spoken of more explicitly. Second, Mary Kay distributors also show how they acquired the success rapidly. Initially, this strategy seems contrary to the enhancement strategy of claiming obstacles make a success more worthy of recognition. I believe this strategy is compelling to the audience for Mary Kay success stories. The distributors in the audience are women who have typically labored long in traditional jobs without attaining the level of success they desire. An individual who succeeds quickly in Mary Kay demonstrates that women are able to succeed if they have the right opportunity. Women can take more than one path to success. Third, Mary Kay distributors acclaim efficient successes. This enhancement strategy is consistent with telling an intelligible woman story that maintains the importance of family. By making "smart money," their achievements remain embedded in their connections to others (Jelinek, 1980). So, while women can proclaim that their achievements are worthy of recognition for the same reasons our culture grants significance to men's success stories, these particular women also acclaim their successes through three unique discursive strategies that are understandable as part of a woman's story of success.

DISCLAIMING DISCOURSE

While distributors want to acclaim their successes, they are constrained by a competing goal of appearing modest. In telling Mary Kay success stories, distributors attend to modesty issues by dissociating themselves from responsibility for the success and by detracting from the significance of the success. The disclaiming discourse closely resembles the strategies used by both Nobel winners and athletes.

Dissociation Strategies

Mary Kay distributors appear modest when they diminish the responsibility for their own success. This is accomplished by

(1) sharing responsibility for the success, (2) attributing the success to uncontrollable and external causes, and (3) expressing surprise at the success or recognition.

Tellers share responsibility for their success. When individuals share responsibility, they allot a portion of the credit for the success to others. They appear unassuming by acknowledging that individual success depends on others. This strategy appears often in the discourse because the Mary Kay culture establishes a supportive community, and the audience for these success stories often includes the very individuals who are being credited.

The Mary Kay culture fosters personal relationships among distributors. Distributors describe their units metaphorically as families and support groups. It is to be expected that successful Mary Kay distributors would primarily share credit with their directors, recruiters, and sister consultants. These women are credited with providing encouragement, advice, information, support, motivation, praise, enthusiasm, optimism, and role models.

Distributors share credit for their successes with their director. She is in a position to influence and help them the most within the Mary Kay organization. Distributors learn that if they do what their director tells them to do, they will become successful. The Queen of Recruiting at the most recent Seminar reveals that she won that honor because "I did what my Director told me to do" (September newsletter, p. 3). Tina, a red jacket on her way to a Mary Kay car, reveals:

> I couldn't do it without Cathy. I mean she's constantly giving me a pep talk. (October 21 interview)

Amy credits her director for providing a role model and the encouragement necessary for the success of each consultant.

> I just think she [Cathy] is an incredible lady. I really do. I mean brilliant in a way but easy to talk to in your unit, you know. So she's just been an incredible role model. If you have a question about anything I always feel like I can call

her. I always feel like she's very encouraging and she believes
in all of us, you know. (October 22 interview)

At the unit level, the director is the most successful woman and
has the most to impart to her distributors. Distributors recognize
her for these contributions and appear modest about their own
role in their successes.

Besides the director, the consultant's recruiter (i.e., the Mary
Kay distributor who signed this person up to become a consultant) can offer advice and support. Fran shares responsibility for her success with her recruiter:

I believe Eloise, who recruited me, has been very supportive.
She is constantly praising me and telling me that I'm doing
all the right things and how proud she is. (November 11
interview)

Thus, Mary Kay consultants give credit to their recruiters for
providing support.

This relationship is reciprocal, for recruiters also recognize
the contributions of their team members to their successes.

My team members. They make me want to keep going. Just
because I have them now and I want to do something with
them. (October 12 interview with Sarah)

Sarah gives credit to her team for motivating her to continue
with her Mary Kay business. As a Mary Kay line (i.e., joined
by relationships to the recruiter with commissions connected
to the productivity of the downline), their economic success is
interdependent.

The members of this unit are connected by complicated
family genealogies originating with recruiters, and they come
together regularly at weekly Success Meetings. The distributors
give credit to other sister consultants.

By having the Monday meetings it keeps you on track. They're
centered to be positive instead of thinking about negative.
It's really funny. I'd go to meetings feeling tired and come
out feeling a lot better. I mean ready to do things. They [the

other consultants present at meetings] are a support group. (October 5 interview with Simone)

Simone's ability to work her Mary Kay business during the week is tied to the support and enthusiasm generated by her sister consultants at these meetings. She credits them with providing her with the support she needs to be successful.

While the credit distributed thus far has been to members of a distributor's particular unit, distributors also share credit with the company (Mary Kay Cosmetics) and with Mary Kay Ash herself. The company is recognized for providing detailed information, particularly in the form of training.

> In a *Career Moves* videotape made available to potential recruits, several successful Mary Kay distributors are featured. Several of these individuals indicate that they were able to learn to be beauty consultants because of the support offered by Mary Kay Inc. This takes the form of conferences and events throughout the year. There is "ongoing training." (Notes on *Career Moves* video)

Mary Kay publications provide information to help consultants succeed.

> Carol says she used the suggestion she found in last month's *Applause* and sent letters to business executives and has three appointments scheduled for them to look at her Christmas baskets to purchase for clients, employees, and family. (November 15 Success Meeting)

The company is acknowledged by Mary Kay distributors as a resource for independent consultants to use on their way to success.

Mary Kay Ash is idolized by distributors. She represents the dream and they see her as central to their own successes.

> As I was expressing my gratefulness to Mary Kay for the difference she has made in my life by her faith, perseverance, and courage to step out of her comfort zone, she took me by

the hand and looked me in the eye and said, "Now it's your
turn to pass it on." (November newsletter, p. 1)

Cathy gives credit to Mary Kay for her own success as a
director. Mary Kay Ash models the qualities Cathy has learned,
and she in turn can model these for her own unit.

Mary Kay Ash sees the company as blessed by God and is
humbled by her small part in the success of the company.

> I believe He [God] used this company as a vehicle to give
> women a chance. And I feel very humble and very fortunate
> to have had a part in showing other women the way. (Ash,
> 1987, p. 8)

Her beliefs are shared by others in the Mary Kay family. Cathy
also credits God with her success:

> How did I do it [become a successful director]? Number one:
> I have God on my side. Seriously I believe that. (December
> 7 interview)

Cathy explains that her success as a director is directly related
to her relationship with God. Her description of the causes of
her success are consistent with a central tenet in Mary Kay that
asserts an ordering of priorities that places "God first, family
second, and career third." God is a partner and oversees a
Mary Kay distributor's success.

Individuals given credit outside of the Mary Kay family are
husbands. Most of the Mary Kay consultants in Cathy's Comets are married. Husbands get credit for offering useful advice
and particularly for providing necessary support.

> And luckily my husband, you know, stands behind me, where
> the kids are concerned, so that I can come out and do my
> classes and I can come to the Mary Kay meetings and go to
> all the functions. (November 15 interview with Lois)

Mary Kay husbands are actively persuaded to be cheerleaders
for their wives (e.g., Mary Kay Cosmetics sponsors events that
include or are directed toward Mary Kay husbands), and it is

widely believed that distributors with supportive husbands are more likely to succeed in the business.

Mary Kay distributors are generous in distributing credit to others. The director, recruiter, sister consultants, God, and husbands are among those described as partially responsible for their individual success. Sharing credit redirects attention from the individual to others and achieves the appearance of modesty.

Tellers attribute their success to external or uncontrollable causes. If success is, in part, the result of causes beyond the control of an individual, direct responsibility for that success is reduced. A Mary Kay distributor can create the impression of modesty by suggesting that her success is caused by timing or the quality of the product.

For example, Mary Kay successes, as well as failures, are attributed to "timing."

> *Q:* What makes the difference between someone who is successful in Mary Kay and someone who is not?
>
> *Sarah:* Honest and truly? I think the bottom line would be timing in their lives. Because you just see too many people quit and come back and be extremely successful the second time. (October 12 interview)

When Mary Kay distributors are successful, the timing is right. Fran suggests that her recent recruiting success is a matter of good timing, but timing that occurs primarily because of chance circumstances:

> Actually, so I don't really think that I can take full credit for this happening [getting a recruit]. It just fell into place. (November 11 interview)

Achieving this important step in Fran's Mary Kay career is attributed largely to chance.

An external cause for Mary Kay success is the quality of the product. Distributors reduce responsibility for their sales successes by arguing that the product sells itself.

> Melinda reports excitedly that she had a $400 class. She tells
> the other consultants that the products just sold themselves.
> (October 27 Success Meeting)

> The product sells itself so well that really it's that initial just
> getting someone to say, "Yes, I'll try it and put it on my
> face." (October 22 interview with Amy)

Amy makes it clear that the beauty consultant does have an
important role in obtaining the sales, but the successes are due,
in part, to the ease in selling the product.

This strategy stands in contrast to explanations of causes
for the purpose of acclaiming. Success is acclaimed when it is
attributed to internal and controllable causes but disclaimed
when it is attributed to external and uncontrollable causes.

*Tellers express surprise at their unexpected success or
recognition.* A Mary Kay distributor appears modest when
she expresses genuine surprise and amazement at her success.
This discursive strategy positions the distributor as modest
because she does not presume success. An individual who
expects success is judged as arrogant, while an individual who
creates a sincere impression of surprise is viewed as unpretentious. In an August newsletter, the remarks of a director who
was in the Queen's Court of Recruiting at Seminar are repro-
duced for consultants:

> Being second runner up to the Queen was certainly a sur-
> prise and an honor. (August-TX newsletter, p. 1)

The success is valued (i.e., described as an honor) and this
director expresses surprise at her good fortune. Tina also expresses astonishment at being a diamond star consultant in the
last quarter:

> Never did I dream I would be a diamond star consultant
> last time but it just worked out that way. (October 21
> interview)

Her success is unexpected and occurs by happenstance. To characterize success as a surprise creates the impression of modesty because it makes it appear that it is less planned, controlled, and expected as a matter of course.

In summary, a Mary Kay distributor can create an impression of modesty in describing her own success by diminishing responsibility for that success. When the success is (1) shared with others, (2) attributed to uncontrollable and external causes, or (3) produces surprise, the consultant is creating discourse that portrays an unassuming self-identity. Prior research has investigated sharing credit with others (Decker, 1987, 1990; Miller, Cooke, Tsang, & Morgan, 1992), external causal explanations (Martinko, Weiner, & Lord, 1995), and the expression of surprise (Miller, Cooke, Tsang, & Morgan, 1992) as strategies for appearing less responsible for an act or less boastful of a success.

Because cultural expectations dissociate women from responsibility for their successes, discourse reducing responsibility is less elaborated than their acclaiming discourse. Like Nobel winners, they share credit with others and express surprise at their success. But Nobel laureates display additional dissociation strategies that are not apparent in the stories of Mary Kay distributors (e.g., complimenting others, expressing gratitude). Nobel laureates can afford to be modest without risking the loss of recognition. Like athletes, Mary Kay distributors share credit, attribute success to external or uncontrollable causes, and express surprise.

Detraction Strategies

Mary Kay distributors create a modest impression by reducing the significance of their individual successes. The achievement is lessened by deflecting attention from the successful individual through (1) a comparison to other accomplishments or (2) characterizing the success as incomplete. Like the dissociation strategies, these detraction strategies were present in previous case studies.

Tellers note their success is less noteworthy compared to other accomplishments. A distributor positions her own success as less noteworthy than other Mary Kay distributors. Distributors downgrade their economic successes (e.g., other consultants win top sales honors more frequently, generate higher sales at classes), status successes (e.g., other distributors become red jackets and directors faster), and personal transformations (e.g., other Mary Kay saleswomen have less difficulty overcoming their fears).

Fran never misses a Success Meeting and always brings a guest. Yet, when she is praised for this accomplishment, she diminishes her own success by focusing on other distributors' economic successes.

> I know people who do the same number of classes I'm doing and they are selling more so I'm not sure why I haven't. What the difference is there . . . I've never had a $300 week and that's my goal and I mean there have been recruits in there—people that have all around me that have done three and five and eight hundred dollar weeks. I've never had those kind of weeks. But I know they will come. (November 11 interview)

Fran selects recent recruits (who are like herself) as her comparison group. Their economic successes are characterized as larger than her own, although she is optimistic that eventually she will have this form of success. Accomplishments are minimized through comparisons.

Tina depicts her own status success as less noteworthy than Mary Kay consultants in other units. She has been with the company for two and a half years, and, despite her considerable successes as a red jacket, Tina describes others' quick ascension to director and Mary Kay cars as more noteworthy.

Q: How long have you been a Mary Kay consultant?

Tina: I've been a consultant about two and one-half years.

Q: So that's not very long.

> *Tina:* But long compared to some people and how they've done—what they've done in their career. As I listen to these tapes [motivational tapes sold by Mary Kay Cosmetics] of some people that have come into the company—within the first four months they won their car, in the first eleven months they became a director. (October 21 interview)

Tina downgrades her own success by choosing to compare herself to Mary Kay distributors featured on motivational tapes. They have surpassed her own success by earning status in the Mary Kay hierarchy more swiftly.

Amy directs attention to other distributors who have been more successful in recruiting:

> She's [Tina] just done so well, getting out there and interviewing people and getting business associates and talking about the company. That's been something that's been really difficult for me—very difficult for me. (October 22 interview)

Amy redirects attention from her sales accomplishments to Tina's successes in recruiting. By comparison, her own efforts appear less remarkable.

Tellers suggest their success is incomplete. Successes thus far are sometimes characterized as a work in progress. To present the work as unfinished diminishes its present significance. There are two senses in which the work is presented as unfinished. First, distributors focus on future goals that have not yet been achieved rather than past goals that have already been accomplished. Second, distributors reveal areas they need to improve before they can truly be successful.

Mary Kay distributors are encouraged to continually set and reset high goals. A director shares her beliefs about the role of goal setting in her own success by adapting a line from a Robert Browning poem:

> One's reach should exceed one's grasp, else what's a heaven for? The goals become my frame of reference for the day. . . . I set high standards for myself. Mary Kay made a speech which

put everything in perspective for me. She said, "Reach for
the moon. Even if you don't succeed you'll land in the stars."
I always have the feeling that I've indeed landed in the stars.
(July newsletter, p. 5)

The Mary Kay culture (even Mary Kay Ash herself) encourages high goals, making this strategy for claiming modesty
readily available to the distributors. At a Mary Kay weekend
retreat, one activity involved writing Mary Kay goals on pil-
lowcases so consultants could contemplate their goals while
they slept.

Cathy has Lois come up to the front and they each hold an
end of the pillowcase Lois made while Lois reads off the
goals she has written: "Be a red jacket, work Mary Kay full
time, do 2 interviews a week, and win a Grand Am by the
Spring of 94." (October 11 Success Meeting)

The success achieved can only be partial because there are
always higher goals to be reached.
    Consultants identify their economic successes as incom-
plete. Becky has had many successful classes and won ribbons
and weekly top sales honors, but she considers these successes
to be unfinished because she does not have a sufficient customer base yet.

I guess I'd just like to mainly have my customer base built
up to where I'm profiting more. (November 8 Interview)

She identifies her success as incomplete because it has not yet
generated the profit she expects from her business.
    In terms of status goals, distributors want to be red jackets,
directors, and national sales directors. Distributors are con-
tinuously working on climbing up the Mary Kay hierarchy.

My short-term goal is to have my red jacket. . . . I want to be
a team leader too, but I have to get my red jacket before I
can be a team leader. (October 22 interview with Amy)

> Well my long-term goals are to win my car and be a director. And right now my goal is to have my car by the end of January because I plan to go on target at the end of this month. And at that point I feel I can be a director in one month. (October 12 interview with Sarah)

By identifying future goals, these women are modest in their assessments of their past accomplishments.

Mary Kay women also set individual goals and deflect attention from previous personal growth by pointing out the areas where they still need to work. Lois is a regular at Success Meetings and displays the go-give spirit, but she highlights individual goals she has not realized:

> I have a problem, even though I write the goals down. I have a tendency to, you know, 'cause everything else comes before what I want . . . and I know I've got to recruit, but that's one of the hardest things for me. (November 15 interview)

Mary Kay distributors are modest about their past successes, pointing to future economic, status, and personal goals that they have yet to realize.

Newsletters, the *Applause* magazine, and Success Meetings are replete with exhortations for success (e.g., hold three classes a week, talk about the Mary Kay opportunity to anyone who gets within three feet, listen to the Mary Kay motivational tapes, make a goals poster, work at the Mary Kay business every day). Distributors are advised to identify their unmet goals and work harder to accomplish them. The consistent message is that anyone can be successful in Mary Kay who follows these instructions. Distributors who have already had some successes deflect attention and appear modest in their attributions by marking the behaviors they ought to be doing (i.e., as specified in Mary Kay culture) but have neglected.

> What I try to do is a class a week and I haven't been good at it. (October 22 interview with Amy)

I've gotten out of it [the habit of listening to motivational tapes] in the last couple of months. And that's one of the things that really does keep you going. (October 12 interview with Sarah)

I know I should be approaching more people and doing it [interviewing possible recruits] more often. (November 1 interview with Elizabeth)

They can do more to be successful. Their successes are incomplete because they have yet to complete their journey to the ideal (Waggoner, 1994).

Mary Kay distributors create the impression of modesty by reducing the significance of their successes. They characterize their success as (1) less noteworthy compared to other accomplishments and (2) incomplete. Both of the previous case studies analyzed in this book displayed these discursive strategies. But, while these strategies are present in the stories of Mary Kay distributors, they are subordinate to the acclaiming discourse.

CONCLUSION

Every Monday night, women in professional dress and carefully applied faces arrive for a Mary Kay Success Meeting. Distributors are given several chances to tell their success stories and be recognized. They win awards, applaud each other enthusiastically, share advice, and celebrate the belief that women can be successful. Their stories bring personal glory to the teller, but they also create expectations that those who are listening can learn how to be successful. Mary Kay distributors are eager to tell and to listen to the success stories of other distributors. They acclaim their successes by magnifying their responsibility and enhancing the importance of their successes. Although acclaiming is central to their stories, they also respond to an expectation to be modest. Their stories demonstrate a delicate interpersonal accomplishment by creating a successful identity within competing goals of self-enhancement and modesty.

6 Conclusion

You must stir it and stump it,
And blow your own trumpet
Or trust me, you haven't a chance.
    —W. S. Gilbert, *Ruddigore*

Modesty is the only sure bait when
you angle for praise.
        —Lord Chesterfield

The success stories of Nobel winners, athletes, and Mary Kay distributors were examined as self-presentational discourse with the competing goals of securing recognition for a desirable act by "blowing your own trumpet" and appearing modest in order to "angle for praise." This chapter begins with a consideration of the complete typology of discursive strategies across success stories in three case studies. Similarities and variations in strategies by situation are then explored. Multiple goals, a comparison to accounts, and some final implications regarding the relationship between success stories and cultural values are the end point of this narrative.

A TYPOLOGY OF DISCURSIVE STRATEGIES IN SUCCESS STORIES

The goals of success stories are instantiated in strategies that address two cardinal issues. The first concerns individual responsibility for a success. Tellers acclaim by presenting themselves as causal agents and disclaim through discourse that loosens the connection between act and agent. A complete typology of entitlement strategies that claim responsibility and of dissociation strategies that minimize responsibility will be discussed. The second issue organizing success stories pertains

TABLE 6.1

A Typology of Entitlement Strategies

1. Tellers recount that they worked hard to earn the success.

2. Tellers report that they persevered in their work.

3. Tellers describe their self-motivation.

4. Tellers show they are willing to take risks.

5. Tellers demonstrate that they accomplished their success independently.

to the significance of the success. Tellers acclaim by emphasizing the importance of their achievements and disclaim by discounting the worth of their accomplishments. The complete typology of enhancement strategies that acclaim and detraction strategies that disclaim from the three case studies are considered.

RESPONSIBILITY FOR THE SUCCESS: ENTITLEMENT AND
DISSOCIATION STRATEGIES

Tellers claim responsibility for success in entitlement strategies and appear modest about their involvement in the success through dissociation strategies. The typology of entitlement and dissociation strategies that emerged inductively from the three case studies can be discussed in terms of attribution theory (House, 1980; Lau, 1984). In entitlements, tellers assert an internal cause for their success by explicitly describing effort and ability. Attribution to effort "involves the assumption of personal responsibility for success" (House, 1980, p. 540). Similarly, "when we speak of ability, we are dealing with a personal attribute that is a relatively enduring characteristic of the person" (House, 1980, p. 543). Table 6.1 lists the entitlement strategies in the success discourse of Nobel winners, athletes, and Mary Kay distributors. When these tellers describe their hard work and perseverance, they are providing audiences with information about the effort they expended to accomplish the success. Descriptions of internal traits—like risk taking, self-

TABLE 6.2

A Typology of Dissociation Strategies

1. Tellers compliment others.
2. Tellers express surprise at their unexpected success or recognition.
3. Tellers share responsibility for their success.
4. Tellers show they are honored or grateful for the recognition.
5. Tellers attribute their success to external or uncontrollable causes.

motivation, and independence—acclaim dispositional abilities connected to successful outcomes. By characterizing success as the product of effort and ability, tellers of success stories make their audiences aware of internal causes for their achievement.

Dissociation strategies minimize responsibility for a success to create the appearance of modesty. The attribution literature confirms that luck and task difficulty are external causes cited for successes and failures (House, 1980; Lau, 1984). In these case studies, athletes attribute their physical performances to chance; Mary Kay distributors refer to timing as an explanation for their successes. The ease of the task appears in the discourse of Mary Kay distributors who assert that the product sells itself. House (1980) argues that attributing a success to an easy task "seems to indirectly suggest that one has high ability while at the same time presenting a picture of modesty" (p. 543). Each of these examples are particular instances of the strategy of attributing a success to external or uncontrollable causes. Table 6.2 presents the typology of dissociation strategies and depicts several dissociation strategies in addition to the one just described. The remaining strategies deflect recognition of the success. Diverting attention from self to others by complimenting or sharing credit externalizes the recognition and treats the success as a collective and social activity instead of an individualistic experience. Showing gratitude and surprise also marks the meaning of success and the rewarding of recognition for a success as a collaborative social activity. An external audience bestows recognition on a recipient who deserves praise by cultural standards for success, and the recipient behaves graciously and modestly in accepting the recognition while disclaiming an expectation of success. Dissociation strategies externalize the success and recognition to create the appearance of modesty for the individual telling the success story.

SIGNIFICANCE OF THE SUCCESS: ENHANCEMENT AND
DETRACTION STRATEGIES

The second fundamental issue present in success stories is an evaluation of the success. Tedeschi and Melburg (1984) explain the self-presentational motivation for addressing the significance of a success:

> Once the person gains credit for the positive event, the amount of approbation and reward that may be associated with such responsibility is directly proportional to the values involved. Thus, the actor may attempt to enhance the value so as to gain greater reward for the self. (p. 42)

Tellers of success stories acclaim their successes by enhancing their value. The summary of enhancement strategies presented in Table 6.3 manifest process and product considerations in explicitly evaluating the merit of the achievement (Vande Berg & Trujillo, 1989).[1] The process of arriving at a success is enhanced by descriptions of a journey fraught with obstacles. In the discourse of Mary Kay distributors, a diverging process of reaching success rapidly and efficiently is also presented as worthy of praise. As tellers use these strategies, they enhance the successful end by affiliation with a desirable means for reaching that end. The product of a success can also be a source of enhancement. Tellers shape audience perceptions of the distinctiveness and desirability of their accomplishment. Distinctive successes favorably compare an individual to others. Tellers who recount that their successes are superior to others or associated with the great individuals in their field are characterizing their success as distinctive. This distinctiveness conveys that the success is both

TABLE 6.3

A Typology of Enhancement Strategies

1. Tellers indicate their success required overcoming obstacles.
2. Tellers demonstrate that their success realized a higher purpose.
3. Tellers associate their success with the achievement of great individuals in the field.
4. Tellers describe their success as the apex of their ability.
5. Tellers show their success may not be repeatable.
6. Tellers show their success was a turning point.
7. Tellers demonstrate that their success is superior to others.
8. Tellers describe their success as fulfilling a dream.
9. Tellers indicate that their success is acquired rapidly.
10. Tellers indicate that their success is acquired efficiently.
11. Tellers show their success is recognized and rewarded by others.

extraordinary and worthy of recognition. A success is desirable when a positive outcome is associated with the success. In this culture, a success that improves the human condition (e.g., realizes a higher purpose), controls the mind/body (e.g., reaches the apex of a person's ability), or secures valued rewards (e.g., receives the recognition of others) is presumptive evidence of the value of the success. Thus, these enhancement strategies embellish the significance of a success by positively evaluating the process or the product of the success.

Detraction strategies diminish the significance of a success to present a modest impression of the individual telling the success story. Table 6.4 provides a summary of the detraction strategies. In these stories, it is the product rather than the process that is reduced in value through the discourse. The successes are claimed to be less distinctive or desirable than assumed by an audience. Tellers describe their successes as less noteworthy compared to other accomplishments. Their success is characterized as incomplete, restricted, and flawed. As a whole, the detraction strategies create a modest self-presentation by focusing on an individual's humility

TABLE 6.4

A Typology of Detraction Strategies

---

1. Tellers note their success is less noteworthy compared to other accomplishments.
2. Tellers suggest their success is incomplete.
3. Tellers argue their success is limited to a narrow specialty.
4. Tellers indicate their success is flawed.

---

regarding the distinctiveness and desirability of the product of success.

ACCLAIMING AND DISCLAIMING DISCOURSE IN CONTEXT

In each of the case studies, tellers of success stories acclaimed and disclaimed. Issues of responsibility and significance were instantiated in 25 discursive strategies. Table 6.5 summarizes the strategies by case study. Six of the strategies were common across the three case studies and provide evidence for cross-situational narrative forms. The remaining strategies reflect variations in the discourse of these Nobel winners, athletes, and Mary Kay distributors. In this section, similarities in strategies are scrutinized before examining variations in contexts.

SIMILARITIES IN DISCURSIVE STRATEGIES

Similarities in discursive strategies for telling a success story imply situated discourse. Narrative *topoi*, recurrent and cross-situational strategies for securing recognition and appearing modest, are available to tellers. This section scrutinizes the six strategies that appear in every case study.

TABLE 6.5

Acclaiming and Disclaiming Discourse by Case Studies

Acclaiming

Case Study

Entitlement

N		M	1.	Tellers recount that they worked hard to earn the success.
N	A	M	2.	Tellers report that they persevered in their work.
	A		3.	Tellers describe their self-motivation.
		M	4.	Tellers show they are willing to take risks.
		M	5.	Tellers demonstrate that they accomplished their success independently.

Enhancement

N	A	M	1.	Tellers indicate their success required overcoming obstacles.
N		M	2.	Tellers demonstrate that their success realized a higher purpose.
	A		3.	Tellers associate their success with the achievement of great individuals in the field.
	A		4.	Tellers describe their success as the apex of their ability.
	A		5.	Tellers show their success may not be repeatable.
	A		6.	Tellers show their success was a turning point.
	A		7.	Tellers demonstrate that their success is superior to others.
	A	M	8.	Tellers describe their success as fulfilling a dream.
		M	9.	Tellers indicate that their success is acquired rapidly.
		M	10.	Tellers indicate that their success is acquired efficiently.
		M	11.	Tellers show their success is recognized and rewarded by others.

Disclaiming

Dissociation

| N | | | 1. | Tellers compliment others. |
| N | A | M | 2. | Tellers express surprise at their unexpected success or recognition. |

(continued)

TABLE 6.5

Acclaiming and Disclaiming Discourse by Case Studies   *(continued)*

Disclaiming

N A M	3.	Tellers share responsibility for their success.
N	4.	Tellers show they are honored or grateful for the recognition.
A M	5.	Tellers attribute their success to external or uncontrollable causes.

Detraction

N A M	1.	Tellers note their success is less noteworthy compared to other accomplishments.
N A M	2.	Tellers suggest their success is incomplete.
N	3.	Tellers argue their success is limited to a narrow specialty.
A	4.	Tellers indicate their success is flawed.

Note. N = Nobel winners
      A = Athletes
      M = Mary Kay distributors

Tellers report that they persevered in their work. Nobel Prize winners persevere for lifetimes in the pursuit of knowledge. Athletes' successes are based on years of practice and competition. Mary Kay distributors refuse to give up and keep recruiting and selling despite personal and professional challenges. Perseverance, as an entitlement strategy, is direct evidence of sustained effort by an individual and claims an internal attribution is appropriate. In this strategy, tellers reflect and reaffirm the cultural values embodied in the work ethic (Biggart, 1983). The cultural value is expressed in a belief that "every individual has a chance of achieving upward mobility through his or her own efforts" (Goldstein & Smucker, 1986, p. 127).

Tellers indicate their success required overcoming obstacles.
The tellers of these stories describe the nature of the obstacles
they faced to enhance their ultimate success. Nobel laureates
battle against negative attitudes (e.g., about the realistic
chances for peace) and the mysteries of science. Athletes describe their problems with competitors, illness, and injuries in
their attempts to master their bodies. Mary Kay distributors
overcome illness, poverty, and negative attitudes in their journey toward success. Like Campbell's (1956) monomyth, the
protagonist demonstrates worthiness by successfully negotiating complicating actions before achieving a meritorious victory. This process of arriving at success is a well-known plot
and entrenched in a cultural value that urges individuals to
pursue success even in the face of incredible obstacles (Merton,
1957b). To achieve success through this process is to enhance
its value.

Tellers share responsibility for their success.   By sharing credit,
a teller reduces personal responsibility for the behavior and
appears modest in recognizing the contributions of others. Nobel
awardees share credit with coworkers, colleagues, mentors, and
spouses. Athletes thank team members, coaches, fans, and God.
Mary Kay saleswomen attribute success, in part, to their director, recruiter, other Mary Kay distributors, God, and spouses.
Although success is generally assumed to be individualistic in
its achievement and its recognition (Slugoski & Ginsburg, 1989),
individuals can appear modest by recognizing that their success
exists within the larger social context. An individual's success
is celebrated as a collective success, and those individuals identified by the teller can share in the recognition.

*Tellers express surprise at their unexpected success or
recognition.*   Nobel Prize winners cannot believe they have
been selected for this prestigious award. Athletes are caught by
surprise when they did not expect to win or to excel in a
performance. Mary Kay distributors express incredulity when
their sales and recruiting performances exceed their expectations.

In cultural beliefs about success, luck plays a part. Successes can be unexpected (Goldstein & Smucker, 1986). Recognition is given by others, to be surprised by this reward is to suggest humility. Where certainty may be perceived as arrogance, uncertainty introduces chance and appropriate amazement at the good fortune.

Tellers note their success is less noteworthy compared to other accomplishments. Tellers detract from their accomplishments by comparing them to other successes. Nobel winners claim that their own discoveries pale in comparison to other scientists. Athletes point to other players in the same sport with greater athletic feats to their credit. Mary Kay distributors recount the stories of other cosmetic queens who have reached success faster, made more money, and gone farther in the Mary Kay hierarchy. The prevalence of comparisons in evaluating behavior and the adaptability of the strategy to any context accounts for its recurrence in these cases.

Tellers suggest their success is incomplete. Detraction from a success can be achieved by focusing on a future goal rather than present accomplishments. Nobel winners continue to probe the mysteries of nature. Athletes focus on the next game or competition. Mary Kay distributors continually strive for the next level on the elaborate status hierarchy. No matter what the success, a new challenge can always be conceived and a present success can be characterized as incomplete. This strategy is consistent with cultural expectations that individuals should not "rest on their laurels" but continue to be productive and successful members of the social structure.

This set of strategies are narrative *topoi* for individuals who are in a position to tell their own success story. The self-presentation of a success is a delicate interpersonal accomplishment because of competing goals to secure recognition and appear modest. These similar strategies suggest that narrative *topoi* are strategic responses to this complicated situation.

VARIATIONS IN DISCURSIVE STRATEGIES

Four of the strategies appear in two of the case studies, but are absent from the third. This may occur because these two contexts share features not held in common with the third or because the stories examined did not create an exhaustive typology for each context. Fifteen of the strategies appear in a single case study and may also reflect either limitations in the stories examined or variations in the contexts selected. A closer examination of these 15 unique strategies probes possible context differences in the strategic choices of tellers.

Nobel Winners

Three strategies are unique to Nobel discourse, and they all disclaim the success. Nobel winners tell their success stories at an elaborate ceremonial occasion in which they receive tremendous praise. Representatives of the Nobel Foundation and Sweden are in the audience. Nobel laureates have less need of acclaiming strategies with this audience, but disclaiming is particularly meaningful discourse (Mulkay, 1984). This public occasion accounts for the appearance of the two unique strategies of complimenting others and of expressing honor or gratitude. Nobel winners compliment Alfred Nobel, the selection committee (who picked them from numerous other possibilities), those organizing the ceremonial occasion, and the people of Sweden in their acceptance addresses. Remarkably, many of those who are complimented are in the audience. Nobel winners also express their gratitude for the recognition. The Nobel Awards are subjective judgments that a particular individual is most worthy of the recognition. A laureate shows gratitude for having been selected from among many deserving candidates for the honor. Furthermore, it is conventional for the recipient to respond to the praise that occurs in a public awards ceremony with a show of gratitude and to compliment the audience (Goffman, 1971). These strategies have self-presentational implications because they avoid self-praise by focusing attention on others rather than the self. A third strategy unique to this context is the detraction strategy of arguing that their success is limited to a narrow specialty. A scientist's reluctance to overstate claims may make these tellers more likely to highlight the limitations of their abilities than the tellers of success stories in other contexts.

Athletes

Seven strategies are unique to the stories told by athletes, and all but one acclaim their success. Sports are inherently competitive and successes are measurable and objective to a larger degree than successes in other contexts. Motivation is necessary to win, and athletes tell their audiences that they possess the ability to motivate themselves. Sports involve constant social comparisons, and the strategies of positive associations with sports legends and claiming supremacy over the competition provide a standard for acclaiming a behavior as distinctive. Claims of supremacy are also more likely in situations where competition is explicitly valued. Acclaiming by identifying a discrete turning point and disclaiming by suggesting a performance was incomplete are consistent with the ability to measure outcomes and objectively evaluate performances by some agreed upon standards. Unlike other contexts, athletes use the strategy of enhancing a success by claiming that opportunities for remaining successes are limited. This may be more likely to occur with athletes because of the very limited time period in which athletes are at their physical peak.

Mary Kay Distributors

Mary Kay distributors used five strategies that were not found in the other contexts, and all of them acclaim success. Gender expectations make it difficult for women to tell a success story about their business accomplishments. Women's successes are perceived as unexpected and attributed to external causes (Deaux & Emswiller, 1974; Giacalone & Riordan, 1990). They must work harder to convince audiences they are entitled to credit for an important success. Mary Kay distributors describe their willingness to take risks to succeed. They are unique in proclaiming that their success is accomplished independently, but they must overcome a cultural expectation that women are dependent on others for their success. Mary Kay distributors acclaim their successes by challenging gender expectations that they will be cautious and dependent. They enhance their success by showing that it is rewarded. In the other case studies, the process of arriving at a success is always described as a journey with obstacles in the path. Mary Kay distributors describe this journey as well, but they also depict a second worthy journey toward success through rapid and efficient ascension. Within the Mary Kay culture, women are often frustrated by traditional jobs that limit their potential for success. They are attracted to the possibility of an alternative route to a quick success. To claim to have taken either journey is a way of enhancing that success.

Tracy and Naughton (1994) contrast two research traditions on interactional strategies. Discourse-analytic approaches rely on knowledge of the culture to interpret the meanings of strategies; communication scholars have identified strategies for accomplishing particular goals. Tracy and Naughton (1994) argue that identity work is "highly situation-bound" (p. 285) and more appropriately investigated by drawing on information from the situation as well as the texts. My analysis suggests that a common purpose, despite other situational variations, produces similar discourse forms. However, the nature of the success, the occasion for telling the story, and the values of the subculture contribute to the situatedness of the talk. I would argue that discursive strategies are influenced and made meaningful by goal and situation.

MULTIPLE GOALS IN SUCCESS STORIES

The previous research on multiple goals frequently involves the competition of instrumental and face goals (Kline, 1985; O'Keefe, 1991; O'Keefe & Shepherd, 1987, 1989). A success story is an opportunity to shape an audience's favorable perception of the teller by negotiating the meaning of an event or behavior. Identity goals compete because a teller wants an audience to give credit for a desirable event but also wants to appear modest. A teller who takes too much credit and brags about the success could be perceived negatively. But tellers who do not claim enough credit for a desirable event by being overly modest can fail to achieve a desirable identity that occurs from having been judged as a success. So how do tellers manage the goals of taking credit but not taking too much and enhancing the success but not making too much of the success?

CONCENTRATION

Competing goals appear in the discourse, but the trade-offs of multiple goals can be managed by concentrating on one goal rather than the other. This is similar to O'Keefe and Shepherd's (1987, 1989; O'Keefe, 1988, 1991) separation strategy in which interactants accomplish multiple goals by attending to both, but do so in different parts of a message. Concentration also implies that one of the goals is more prominent in the discourse. The Nobel discourse is characterized by a more developed repertoire of strategies for disclaiming. The award itself carries information about the laureates' responsibility and the importance of the contribution. The audience has extensive knowledge of the success (Baumeister & Jones, 1978; Schlenker & Leary, 1982), elicits the success story, and provides a ceremonial occasion for the enactment of praise that leads to an emphasis on disclaiming (Mulkay, 1984). Athletes' and Mary Kay distributors' stories include an extensive repertoire of acclaiming discourse. The competitive and impermanent nature of sports successes heighten the importance of acclaiming. Within the Mary Kay culture, the struggle to be recognized as successful women despite cultural expectations provides distributors with a compelling reason to stress their accomplishments at weekly Success Meetings and to concentrate on acclaiming discourse.

CONVERGENCE

In convergence, competing goals are joined within strategies that simultaneously acclaim and disclaim. These messages do not transcend competing goals like O'Keefe and Shepherd's (1987, 1989; O'Keefe, 1988, 1991) integration strategy, but more closely resemble Pomerantz' (1978) discourse solutions when interactants face multiple constraints. A reexamination of some of the strategies illustrates convergence. The dissociation strategy of sharing responsibility with others distributes partial credit to others. But the remainder of the credit implicitly belongs to the teller and functions as an entitlement. By complimenting others, a teller redirects attention through shifting part of the attention from the self to others (Pomerantz, 1978). The redirected praise indirectly acknowledges acceptance of the recognition for the success. Similarly, indicating feelings of honor or gratitude for the recognition presupposes the teller's acknowledgment of the importance of the success. Although each of these strategies involves some convergence between the goals of securing recognition and appearing modest, one goal can be argued to be more direct.

Telling a success story is a delicate interpersonal accomplishment. The two superordinate strategies of concentration and convergence illustrate interactants' achievements in managing competing identity goals while telling a success story. The addition of concentration and convergence to O'Keefe and Shepherd's (1987, 1989) three strategies of selection, separation, and integration extends the analysis of multiple goals and gives explicit attention to competing identity goals.

ACCLAIMING, DISCLAIMING,
AND ACCOUNTING

In contrast to acclaiming, the literature on accounting is extensive, and the typologies of account strategies are well developed. The status of acclaiming as the counterpart of
accounting suggests possible parallels. Whether the event in
question is desirable or undesirable, the issues central to any
self-presentation are the actor's responsibility and the significance of the event. Accounting for a problematic event evokes
attempts to minimize responsibility (i.e., excuses) and the
failure aspects of the event (i.e., justifications). Acclaiming a
desirable event attempts to maximize responsibility (i.e.,
entitlements) and the success aspects of the event (i.e., enhancements) (Schlenker, 1980; Tedeschi & Melburg, 1984;
Tedeschi & Norman, 1985; Tedeschi & Riess, 1981a). Acclaiming could be expected to contrast with accounting. Entitlement strategies are compared to excuses, and enhancement
strategies are related to justifications.

The acclaiming discourse describing work and perseverance as entitlements imply productive activity toward the goal
of success, while failures are excused by referencing human
shortcomings that account for problematic events (Schönbach,
1980). If the teller of a success story encounters an obstacle in
the process of reaching a success, it is mastered and described
to enhance that success in acclaiming rather than being used as
an excuse in accounting. One who accounts for a problematic
event may choose to admit helplessness in dealing with the
situation and attribute failure to external causes, but the teller
of the success story recounts personality characteristics (i.e.,
willingness to take risks; self-reliance) as evidence of an internal attribution for their success. Both enhancements and justifications address the evaluation of an event. In acclaiming,
enhancements describe the desirable nature of the process and
product of the success. In accounting, justifications minimize
the undesirable aspects of the event by denying and minimizing
the damage (Schönbach, 1980). Tedeschi and Riess (1981b)
develop a typology of appeals underlying justifications. Ap-

peals to humanistic values are similar to acclaims that a higher purpose is achieved by an individual's success. They also point to the use of social comparisons, and these strategies are inherent in enhancements that assert supremacy over others and association with great individuals in the field. Despite these few similarities, the enhancement strategies are quite distinct from justifications. The grounds for arguing that a behavior is desirable are not the opposite of those that argue a behavior should not be interpreted as undesirable. For example, a teller can enhance a success by explaining that it fulfills a dream, but an individual accounting for an undesirable behavior is unlikely to use the absence of achieving a dream as relevant grounds for justifying the behavior.

Disclaiming discourse might be expected to be more similar to accounts than acclaiming discourse. While dissociations minimize responsibility for a desirable event to appear modest, excuses minimize responsibility to avoid blame. Of the dissociation strategies, attributing behavior to external causes is similar to an excuse. Sharing credit with others loosens the connection between act and agent just as shifting the blame operates as an account strategy (Benoit, 1995; Schönbach, 1990). Expressing surprise at the success shares the element of chance with the account strategy of claiming accidental causes (Scott & Lyman, 1968). Detractions lead to a judgment that the act was not as good as might be perceived (e.g., the performance was flawed or the success was incomplete), while justifications account for why the act was not as bad as it appeared. The use of comparisons to make judgments about the act (Tedeschi & Riess, 1981b) also parallels transcendence (Benoit, 1995).

A comparison of acclaiming, disclaiming, and accounting is productive at the broadest levels. However, acclaims are not simply the logical opposition of accounts. While disclaiming is closer to account strategies, the remedial nature of accounts make the strategies quite distinct from those used to tell a success story. For example, the strategies of sharing credit with others and shifting the blame redistribute responsibility but remain distinct at another important level. In sharing credit, others are being recognized for positive influences, and the teller of the success story redistributes partial credit. When a speaker shifts the blame, others are being singled out for their negative influence, and the speaker benefits most from a complete redistribution of the blame.

SUCCESS STORIES AND CULTURAL VALUES

Cultural values are displayed in success stories. These values shape the kind of success story that can be told intelligibly. The influence of cultural values on the kinds of stories told was most apparent in the analysis of the stories of Mary Kay distributors. Because their success challenges cultural expectations for women, the work of redefining their stories to be intelligible was striking. Economic successes were redefined as acts of caring and affirmations of family. Status successes were recast to exist within a female hierarchy that did not challenge patriarchy. Personal successes involved a transformation that feminized traditionally masculine traits and abilities linked to success while maintaining feminine values like cooperation. Women's stories focused on acclaiming to counter gender expectations that their successes were dependent on others and are trivial. In contrast to the case study of Mary Kay distributors, the meanings of success appeared explicit and unquestioned for Nobel winners and athletes because they reaffirmed cultural values. Their stories were intelligible without redefinition, but I would argue that their stories are also constrained by cultural expectations and expressions of ideology (DuPlessis, 1985; Gergen, 1992).

The stories of Nobel winners are primarily the narratives of scientists. Cultural values about science and the scientific enterprise are conveyed in these success stories (as distinct from those stories told by winners of the Literature and Peace Prizes). Science is often assumed to be superior to other forms of knowing. Science has produced results and can demonstrate progress. Laureates employ the belief that science improves the human condition through knowledge of the world by arguing their discoveries serve this higher purpose. The stories reinforce a belief that science is cumulative as winners compliment those who have made important contributions in their fields prior to their own successes. Individualism is endorsed in these stories because the awards are presented and accepted by individuals rather than the research teams common in most scientific fields. Science is also presented in these success stories as a cooperative enterprise. The Nobel discourse is marked by the absence of "any trace at all of the prejudice, bitterness, or competition which appears persistently in scientists', including Nobel Prizewinners', descriptions of their careers in other contexts" (Mulkay, 1984, p. 544; Brannigan, 1981; Knorr-Cetina, 1981; Latour & Woolgar, 1979). These stories are told exclusively by men in this sample and reflect the limited expectations for women in science that mirror the position of women in traditionally male occupations within the culture at large (McCain & Segal, 1982). Nobel winners tell success stories that reflect cultural values held about science and the nature of the scientific enterprise.

The stories of athletes reflect the "symbolic expression of the values of the larger political and social milieu" (Lipsky, 1975, p. 351). Competition is overtly endorsed and this means there are clear winners and losers. Successes can be objectified and quantitatively measured (Trujillo, 1991). In enhancing their successes, athletes claim they performed better than the competition and executed perfect performances. Their stories are about individuals who play the game for enjoyment and realize their personal dreams through hard work. Sports as a business is noticeably absent in these particular stories. Athletes' stories, with the collaboration of sportswriters, idealize players and the institution of sports in reaffirming cultural values.

Tellers' stories are complicated by oppositional values in the culture (Trujillo & Ekdom, 1985) such as hard work and luck; predictable outcomes and unexpected results; individualism and collective effort; competition and cooperation; and the difficulty journey and the quick success. Despite their apparent inconsistency, these opposing values are endorsed and displayed in and across this collection of success stories. In acclaiming, tellers demonstrate that they worked hard and persevered to achieve success. But they also tell stories about external or uncontrollable causes for their successes (e.g., luck). Success is partly controllable and uncontrollable. If success is internal, stable, and controllable, it becomes predictable. But when tellers express surprise at a success or recognition, they affirm that events can occur by chance. Acclaiming strategies identify the actions taken by individuals to reach success, and tellers of success stories indicate they achieved the outcome independently. However, they also credit others with partial responsibility for the success, and the value of the team is endorsed. Competition and establishing supremacy over competitors motivates achievement. But cooperation is endorsed as a way of helping others succeed and creating a team effort. The journey toward success may encounter obstacles. A success achieved by taking this extended journey is highly valued, but so is the success that is rapid and efficient. The play of oppositional values varies by context. For example, competition and cooperation exist in the stories of athletes, but competition dominates. In the stories of Mary Kay distributors, cooperation is the more dominant of the oppositional values. Success is not a unidimensional concept nor are success stories the simple recountings of events with invariable values.

CONCLUSION

This concluding chapter includes a discussion of the complete typology of strategies tellers use for the self-presentation of success. Narrative *topoi* are elaborated and variations in strategies are accounted for in the stories of Nobel winners, athletes, and Mary Kay distributors. Implications for interpersonal interactions with multiple goals, the account literature, and the relationship between a success story and cultural values have also been considered.

Success is a cultural preoccupation. The self-presentation of success is fundamental to interpersonal communication. These success stories create and negotiate successful identities while managing the competing goals of securing recognition and appearing modest. I hope that this book has integrated the diverse literature on self-presentation and made a convincing argument that scholars should be more interested in self-presentation and discursive strategies for describing desirable events. The goal of this book was to develop a typology of discursive strategies for telling success stories and to display the complexity of this interpersonal accomplishment by examining the influence of multiple goals and situations.

We have opportunities to shape others' impressions of us when we tell our success stories. This week a former student stopped by my office to report that he had been admitted to law school. Steve Forbes celebrated his victory in the 1996 Republican Presidential primary in Arizona. My daughter scored high on a particularly difficult geometry test. And I finished a book. Have I explained that I think this book is important because it opens a rich area of research but the book is incomplete? Research on the effects of these strategies, the influence of goals and situations, and critical analyses of this discourse are specific types of work that need to be pursued in the future. Or did I mention that many other people have influenced my thinking and have been supportive in completing this book? I can tell a lengthy story. What are your success stories and how are they told?

Notes

CHAPTER 1. SELF-PRESENTATION AND THE SUCCESS STORY

1. Any definition of success is dependent on cultural values. The definition in this chapter is meant to reflect Western cultural values implied by the meaning of success.

2. In the social science literature, self-presentation (Arkin & Baumgardner, 1986; Baumeister, 1982; Hogan, Jones, & Cheek, 1985; Jones & Pittman, 1980; Schlenker, 1982; Schlenker & Wiegold, 1992; Schneider, 1981), illusions (Baumeister, 1989), impression regulation (Schlenker & Wiegold, 1992), impression management (Arkin, 1981; Leary & Kowalski, 1990; Schlenker & Wiegold, 1992; Schneider, 1981), self-identification (Schlenker, 1982, 1986), self-interpretation (Cheek & Hogan, 1983), self-promotion (Godfrey, Jones, & Lord, 1986), and ingratiation (Baumeister, 1982; Godfrey, Jones, & Lord, 1986; Jones, 1964) are related terms but reflect differences in the scope of the definition, the function of the behavior, and intended audience for the behavior. In the context of success stories, self-presentation is the most appropriate concept.

3. This language does not imply that self-presentations are always conscious. This issue is controversial. At one extreme, self-presentational behaviors are considered primarily unconscious (Godfrey, Jones, & Lord, 1986; Leary & Kowalski, 1990). At the other extreme, self-presentations are conceived as goal-directed, intentional, and consciously enacted (Hogan, Jones, & Cheek, 1985; Schlenker, 1982). A moderate position suggests self-presentational behaviors may be intentional though not conscious (Tedeschi &

Riess, 1981a; Kellerman, 1992). Self-presentational behaviors are strategic because they are powerful and responsive to situational variations even without the assumption of consciousness (Kellerman, 1992). With repeated use, behaviors may become scripted (Schlenker, 1985) or involve implicit learning with knowledge being "acquired implicitly, held tacitly, and used unconsciously" (Kellerman, 1992, p. 294). The definition of self-presentation presented in this chapter assumes that discourse is enacted strategically to accomplish the goal of creating a positive identity but the situation influences the level of conscious awareness of the self-presentation.

4. The literature on accounts is extensive and describes phases of an account sequence (Buttny, 1977; Cody & McLaughlin, 1985; Goffman, 1967; Schönbach, 1990), details the applications of accounts (Benoit, 1995; Buttny, 1993; Gonzales, Pederson, Manning, & Wetter, 1990; McLaughlin, Cody, & Rosenstein, 1983; Metts & Cupach, 1989; Schlenker & Darby, 1981; Schönbach, 1990), and investigates the effectiveness of particular account types (Blumstein, Carssow, Hall, Hawkins, Hoffman, Ishem, Maurer, Spens, Taylor, & Zimmerman, 1974; Giacalone & Rosenfeld, 1984; Hale, 1986, 1987; Holtgraves, 1989, 1992; Riordan & Marlin, 1987; Riordan, Marlin, & Gidwani, 1988; Riordan, Marlin, & Kellogg, 1983; Weiner, Amirkhan, Folkes, & Verette, 1987).

5. Conformity is valued for the outcomes it makes possible rather than as an end in itself. Job candidates who believe a personnel manager hires disliked employees will express dissimilar attitudes (Jellison & Gentry, 1978).

6. The literature on attributions regarding success and gender is extensive (see Cash, Gillen, & Burns, 1977; Deaux & Emswiller, 1974; Deaux & Farris, 1977; Deaux & Major, 1987; Deaux & Taynor, 1973; Feather & Simon, 1975; Riger & Galligan, 1980).

CHAPTER 2. WINNING THE PRIZE

1. Texts from Nobel acceptance addresses are referenced by the name of the Nobel laureate, the year, the nature of the prize, and the page number of the address in the Nobel Foundation's *Les Prix Nobel*.

2. Descriptions of the work recognized by the Nobel Awards were obtained from Schlessinger and Schlessinger (1991).

3. Dissociation strategies, however, are more prevalent than entitlement strategies in the Nobel discourse. See the discussion section for further development.

4. There have been public disputes regarding the failure of the Nobel committees to award the prize to researchers involved in work being recognized. For instance, Dominique Stéhelin wrote an open letter to the Nobel committee and went public with his complaints that he should have been included in the Nobel Prize awarded to Bishop and Varmus for work in molecular biology. But, these disputes have no place at the presentation

ceremony. In this context, there is no disagreement about the allocation of responsibility for the work.

5. Laureates are not the only ones to tell the Nobel success story. Zuckerman (1977) lists 10 ways institutions (primarily universities) attempt to get some of the credit for Nobel Prizes. If the winner completed undergraduate work or graduate work; studied but did not complete a degree; did postdoctoral work; served on the faculty, before, during, or after receiving the prize; was present at an institution when the award was made or after the award; or served as a visiting professor after the award, an institution is likely to engage in its own entitlement strategies.

CHAPTER 3. THE THRILL OF VICTORY

1. The media is criticized as active participants in the perpetuation of hegemonic masculinity (Brummett & Duncan, 1992; Goldlust, 1987; Nelson, 1980; Trujillo, 1991; Whitson, 1990), the dream myth (Goldlust, 1987), and the commodification of sporting events (Duncan & Brummett, 1991; Jhally, 1989; Trujillo, 1991, 1992; Wenner, 1989).

CHAPTER 4. COSMETIC QUEENS IN PINK CADILLACS

1. Particular Success Meetings and interviews are referenced by the date of their occurrence. These dates are used as organizing features in the field notes.

CHAPTER 6. CONCLUSION

1. Vande Berg and Trujillo (1989) argue that sportswriters describe process when a sports team is losing and product when it is winning. In contrast, the stories told by successful individuals enhance their achievements by characterizing both process and product as desirable.

Appendix

This appendix provides additional methodological details about the ethnographic procedures underlying the analyses presented in chapters 4 and 5.

INCEPTION AND SOCIAL RELATIONS

CHOICE OF SOCIAL SETTING

I chose to observe Mary Kay Success Meetings and interview members of a Mary Kay unit because my previous analyses of success stories were dominated by narratives authored by men. Virtually all Mary Kay distributors are women, and the unit I observed was entirely made up of women (and accounts for my use of feminine pronouns in the text of chapters 4 and 5).

SECURING COOPERATION

One of my acquaintances sold Mary Kay and she told me her group was quite successful. She gave me the name of the director and the meeting times. I called the director and explained that I was working on a book about success stories and was interested in observing Mary Kay meetings. I assured her I would change the names of individuals in any written reports and she invited me to attend the next meeting.

ROLE IN THE SETTING

One of the regular features of a Mary Kay meeting are the introductions. Each woman introduces herself to the group and may tell some information about herself or her successes during the week. At the first meeting I attended, I sat next to my acquaintance. She introduced me as her guest and Cathy, the director, asked me to explain to the distributors why I was observing the meeting. I described my interest in researching the success experiences of women, and she welcomed me to the group. This explanation was called for and repeated for nearly two months and then became abbreviated. My acquaintance did not attend after my initial meeting because of a time conflict and a later decision to become inactive (was no longer selling the product or attending the meetings) in Mary Kay. I began to sit with different women in the audience of consultants at each meeting and engaged them in conversation. While I had an outsider role, I tried to be an active participant in meetings without assuming the role of a consultant. I clapped for distributors who won awards, I congratulated women at the end of meetings on weekly accomplishments, and I offered to provide Christmas decorations for a Mary Kay Christmas open house. The relationships and trust developed over time. I came to know all of the regulars quite well. They greeted me, talked freely about Mary Kay and other topics, and invited me to attend their social gatherings.

GETTING ALONG IN THE SETTING

Cathy came to describe me as a "regular guest" at meetings. This role provided me with a place within the group that both distinguished me from the consultants and explained my presence. Cathy introduced me to Mary Kay guest speakers from other units, enthusiastically greeted me at the beginning of each meeting, and always made sure I had been introduced in the meetings. I did not sense any distrust, but my lengthy presence was unexpected. The women were delighted I was writing about them and would ask about my progress.

Within this unit, one subgroup had a distinct presence. They sat together in the front row and identified themselves as being members of Francine's unit rather than Cathy's unit. It became apparent later that Francine resided in another state and was one of Cathy's offspring directors. Initially, I sensed more misgivings from this subgroup than other members. I found it more difficult to initiate talk with some of these women because most of their interactions were with each other. I made a special effort to interact with these women and eventually interviewed three distributors from this subgroup. After the interviews, I found that whatever misgivings I had sensed earlier had dissipated.

PRIMARY INFORMANTS

During early observations, Simone, one of the consultants who attended meetings regularly, was friendly and cooperative, and I found myself asking her to clarify activities that occurred in the meeting. She would routinely ask me if I understood various terms and contests, and she was extremely valuable in providing background information and directing me to written resources about the company. At this time, she was doing Mary Kay full time, but as the study progressed, she decided to take a traditional job and did not attend meetings as regularly. At that time, I began to develop a relationship with June. She became an essential informant because she knew virtually everyone in the group and was loquacious. Our relationship initially developed because she gave me a facial when her guest didn't show up before the Success Meeting. I began to purchase Mary Kay products from her. This increased the contact between us, and we began to have lunch about once a month. I asked her for confirmation of preliminary claims; she clarified the family genealogy of the distributors within the unit and provided details of implicit rules and meanings. On two occasions, she expressed concern about what she was telling me and would report that she'd shared this concern with Cathy. Cathy had assured her that her conversations with me were appropriate. At the time, I felt the information she'd provided had been primarily descriptive. She may have worried that some of her comments would reflect negatively on the unit or herself. I continued to maintain this relationship after I ceased attending Success Meetings to sustain the opportunity to reenter the setting and conduct additional member checks as the project neared completion.

SOCIAL BLUNDERS

I committed a social blunder at the very first meeting. I had read Mary Kay's autobiography and knew that "professional" dress was expected at the Success Meetings. I dressed carefully for the first meeting, wearing my new red suit. Status in the Mary Kay hierarchy is identified, in part, by clothing. The director has the exclusive right to wear the "director's suit." This suit changes each year, is tailored to the measurements of the director, and is previewed at Seminar. In 1993, the suit was a salmon pink. One level of distributors, red jackets, wear a black skirt, white blouse, and red suit jacket ordered from the company. I had wanted to blend in to the background of the first meeting but had inadvertently worn the "uniform" distinguishing a red jacket. I didn't wear the red suit again.

SERVICES RENDERED FOR PARTICIPATION

I was limited in services I could offer to members of this group in exchange for allowing me to observe meetings and interview members. I tried to be helpful in pouring coffee, cleaning up after meetings, helping a red jacket hang a poster, letting a consultant borrow items for the Christmas open house, and purchasing Mary Kay products. I made arrangements to meet the women I interviewed at restaurants for coffee or lunch and assumed responsibility for the bills. When I felt I'd completed the observations, I let Cathy know it would be the last meeting I attended. I brought inspirational cards for each person with a thank-you message and chocolates. They surprised me by giving me a card they had all signed and a large imitation diamond ring, like the Cinderella gifts the company has become noted for awarding its distributors.

PRIVATE FEELINGS

I felt frustrated by the "dress code" at the meetings. I would often come home from a day at work and have to "redress" before I could go to the meeting. I found myself wearing more makeup than usual to fit in to the group.

I genuinely liked the women I met in this group. While many came from different backgrounds than my own, I found them to be warm and approachable. But after only a few meetings, they began to recruit me to become a Mary Kay consultant. Initially, I tried to reject these overtures through light banter, but several of the consultants became direct and serious about the Mary Kay opportunity. It was clear that my "no" was always interpreted as a "maybe." They could not understand how I could spend so much time at their meetings and not become a consultant. While I recognized that their attempts to recruit me were indications that I was accepted within their community, I found this frustrating because I did not want to jeopardize the relationships I had formed by continually rejecting these overtures. As a researcher I valued the active observer role I had negotiated and did not want to jeopardize this role by becoming a member. Furthermore, as an individual, I did not want to become a Mary Kay consultant.

DATA GATHERING

I observed weekly meetings of Cathy's Comets for five months. The group met on Monday evenings in a conference room at an upscale hotel. There were three separate events that occurred routinely. At 5:45 p.m. some of the distributors would arrive and set up Mary Kay trays for guests they had invited to model for a demonstration of the Mary Kay product. Guests arrived at 6:00 p.m. and a Mary Kay representative (typically a red jacket) would lead the training demonstration for the evening. At the conclusion, guests would be invited by the director to stay for the Success Meeting. As the demonstration concluded, other distributors began to arrive for the Success Meeting. The meeting began at 7:00 p.m. and usually lasted until 9:00 p.m. A social event in the hotel restaurant followed and concluded around 10:00 p.m. Only some of the women stayed for this event, and regulars often attended. Guests who stayed for the Success Meeting and particularly those who had shown interest in the Mary Kay opportunity were encouraged to adjourn to the restaurant. The marketing plan was given to guests, plans were made for upcoming Mary Kay events, and socializing took place at these events. I observed 10 demonstrations and 11 meetings and attended 7 after-meeting events. I also was present at three special Mary Kay events that occurred during regular meeting times (Christmas Open House, Hollywood Glamour Night, and a Glamour Night).

I took extensive written notes during the demonstrations and Success Meetings. During the demonstrations, guests and consultants were occupied with applying products and I could sit in the back and unobtrusively take notes. At the meetings, consultants often took notes, and Cathy provided paper and pencils for special presentations and so my note-taking was not out of place. However, I took more notes than others in the meeting, and there were occasionally comments about what I could possibly be writing down all the time. In order to preserve the detail of the field notes, they were expanded and entered into the computer the next morning. To have taken notes at the social event after meetings would have been very conspicuous because no one else was taking notes and we were at extremely close quarters at the table. My observations at these events were briefly recorded after I returned home. As a result, these notes reflect key threads and stories rather than the detail captured in the field notes of the Success Meetings. At the lunches I had with June for the purpose of member checking, my note-taking was extensive if I was asking for confirmation of preliminary conclusions or if she was providing details that I had not previously heard, but most of the notes from these lunches were written after the event. Exposure to other events or thinking about the setting would periodically prompt some recollection that had not been entered in the original field notes, and these were added at a later time with an appropriate notation. The field notes emphasize concrete descriptions of persons, environments, and actions. They are replete with question marks indicating an incomplete understanding at that point in the observations. Personal reactions as well as preliminary conclusions received special notations in the field notes.

INTERVIEWS

After I attended Mary Kay Success Meetings for a month, I began a series of interviews with 13 distributors. I was interested in interviewing women who were perceived as regulars and successful within the group. I used prior observations of women who were often in front receiving awards during Success Meetings to initially select distributors for interviews. As I interviewed these women, I asked them to identify others who were successful in the unit and began to include these women in the interviews. I purposefully included interviews with women at different levels in the Mary Kay hierarchy. I talked with two directors, four red jackets, and seven consultants. These women had been Mary Kay distributors from four months to 17 years. One of the women had become inactive prior to the interview. Each of the women I approached about an interview was willing to meet with me, and several were flattered I was interested in interviewing them. I took extensive notes during the interviews in addition to tape-recording the interactions. The notes proved helpful in several instances where the background noise of the restaurant reduced the fidelity of the recording. I transcribed verbatim all but one of the interviews (a graduate student completed the other), and these were usually completed within a few days of their occurrence. Prior to the interviews, I developed a set of 10 questions, 9 of which were open-ended. The questions asked were (1) How long have you been a Mary Kay consultant? (2) How did you get started? (3) What has been your major accomplishment in Mary Kay so far? (4) How were you able to accomplish this? Do you have some qualities as a person that were important to this success? (5) How important have other people been to your success? (6) Have you faced obstacles to success in Mary Kay? (7) What are your short-term and long-term goals in Mary Kay? (8) Cathy said that thousands come through the Mary Kay door and go out again. Why have you stayed? What makes the difference between those who are successful and those who aren't? (9) What does it mean to be successful in Mary Kay? (10) Who else would you point to as successful in Mary Kay?

Each interviewee was asked this standard set of questions, but additional questions developed as the interview unfolded and the order of the questions varied. The interviews often provided an opportunity to verify my understandings of the setting.

LITERATURE

Observations and interviews were supplemented with literature produced by the director (newsletters) and Mary Kay Inc. (pamphlets, books, audiotapes, videotapes) as well as articles written by external sources about Mary Kay Cosmetics. These materials were described and logged in the field notes.

DATA ANALYSIS

I assumed at the onset of the project that success in Mary Kay was equivalent to wealth. My original purpose was to describe the discursive practices of success stories. As I reflected on the observations and interviews I was collecting, it became clear that while the meaning of success within this community included prosperity, it was more complex than wealth and would need to be addressed explicitly prior to an analysis of discursive practices for acclaiming success. The definitions of success became the subject of chapter 4.

ETHNOGRAPH, a text-based computer program, was utilized for storage and retrieval of data related to definitions of success. The constant comparative method was used in the coding process, and theoretical memoing was extensive. For the purposes of chapter 4, the first step involved generating a set of categories of meanings of success by comparing instances excerpted from the observations and interviews to each of the categories. The second step involved characterizing the properties of the categories (i.e., meanings of success). Prosperity as success was formulated early in the observations. The theme of status as success was problematic because I wanted (quite unrealistically) for this theme to be discrete from prosperity as success. Only when I could conceptualize this second sense of success as combinatorial was I able to refine the analysis. As an outsider, I recognized the socialization process in Success Meetings early in my observations, but it required additional observations and the interviews to elaborate the transformation expected of Mary Kay distributors and to realize that this was another meaning of success in this community. The last step involved the integration of a theoretical framework. I came to understand that prosperity was redefined to be more acceptable. Making money was perceived as an act of caring and a way of preserving the priority of the family. Rosenwald and

Ochberg's (1992) edited volume on the cultural politics of narratives was useful in extending my analysis of the redefinition of Mary Kay success narratives to each of the meanings of success. In chapter 5, success stories that were about the teller's experiences were isolated for the analysis of acclaiming and disclaiming discourse. The stories were coded for discursive strategies, and often a single recounting of a success contained multiple strategies. The strategies were inductively derived through the constant comparison method. The initial codes were refined as each instance of a particular strategy was compared to other cases. The discourse was coded and sorted with the ETHNOGRAPH program and further refined to obtain a meaningful fit.

MEMBER CHECKING

I used my primary informant, June, to do member checking. She read drafts of the chapters and agreed with the descriptions of the activities with some minor exceptions. For example, June thought I had been extreme in my initial description of the group as "cheering wildly" during meetings because it made the women appear rowdy. She thought the meetings were "loud but dignified." I changed the description to indicate simply that the audience clapped and cheered. June did recall that she was surprised at the boisterous meetings when she first attended, but she assured me that the Success Meetings were now more refined.

CAVEATS

The description is my story about this Mary Kay unit. It is simply an interpretation of the activities and discourse.

The episodes described in the weekly Success Meeting are particular to this unit, this director, and this time period. Sue, one of Cathy's offspring directors, described how she modeled many of the aspects of her meetings after Cathy's but had adapted some features to her own distributors (November 3 interview). In completing member checking, June called to my attention that many things had changed since I had last attended a Success Meeting. Cathy no longer gave ribbons, the pearls/spacers had been replaced by crystals that could be strung on a necklace or turned in for other gifts, the group met at its own training center, the group's demographics had changed to include younger (mid twenties and thirties) women, and conducted Pacesetter classes for those interested in accelerating their progress (January 26 interview).

References

Agins, T. (1992, May 22). Sports stars' earnings. *The Wall Street Journal*, p. B5.

Arkin, R. M. (1980). Self-presentation. In D. M. Wegner & R. R. Vallacher (Eds.), *The self in social psychology* (pp. 158–182). London: Oxford University Press.

———. (1981). Self-presentation styles. In J. T. Tedeschi (Ed.), *Impression management theory and social psychological research* (pp. 311–333). New York: Academic Press.

Arkin, R. M., Appleman, A. J., & Berger, J. M. (1980). Social anxiety, self-presentation, and the self-serving bias in causal attributions. *Journal of Personality and Social Psychology, 38*, 23–45.

Arkin, R. M., & Baumgardner, A. H. (1986). Self-presentation and self-evaluation: Processes of self-control and social control. In R. F. Baumeister (Ed.), *Public and private self* (pp. 75–98). New York: Springer-Verlag.

Arkin, R. M., Cooper, H., & Kolditz, T. (1986). A statistical review of the literature concerning the self-serving attribution bias in interpersonal influence. *Journal of Personality, 48*, 435–448.

Arkin, R. M., & Shepperd, J. A. (1990). Strategic self-presentation: An overview. In M. J. Cody & M. L. McLaughlin (Eds.), *The psychology of tactical communication* (pp. 175–193). Clevedon: Multilingual Matters.

Aronson, E., & Linder, D. (1965). Gain and loss of esteem as determinants of interpersonal attraction. *Journal of Experimental Social Psychology, 1*, 156–171.

183

Ash, M. K. (1984). *On people management.* New York: Warner Books.

———. (1987). *Mary Kay* (2nd ed.). New York: Harper & Row.

Baaten, D. O., Cody, M. J., & DeTienne, K. B. (1993). Account episodes in organizations: Remedial work and impression management. *Management Communication Quarterly, 6,* 219–250.

Banks, J., & Zimmerman, P. R. (1987). The Mary Kay way: The feminization of a corporate discourse. *Journal of Communication Inquiry, 11,* 85–99.

Baskett, G. D. (1973). Interview decisions as determined by competency and attitude similarity. *Journal of Applied Psychology, 57,* 343–345.

Baumeister, R. F. (1982). A self-presentational view of social phenomena. *Psychological Bulletin, 91,* 3–26.

———. (1989). The optimal margin of illusion. *Journal of Social and Clinical Psychology, 8,* 176–189.

Baumeister, R. F., & Jones, E. E. (1978). When self-presentation is constrained by the target's knowledge: Consistency and compensation. *Journal of Personality and Social Psychology, 36,* 608–618.

Belorussian piles up gold. (1992, August 3). *Columbia Daily Tribune,* p. 10B.

Benoit, W. L. (1995). *Accounts, excuses, and apologies: A theory of image restoration strategies.* Albany, NY: State University of New York Press.

Berscheid, E., & Walster, E. H. (1978). *Interpersonal attraction* (2nd ed.). Reading, MA: Addison-Wesley.

Biggart, N. W. (1983). Rationality, meaning, and self-management: Success manuals, 1950–1980. *Social Problems, 30,* 298–311.

———. (1989). *Charismatic capitalism: Direct selling organizations in America.* Chicago: University of Chicago Press.

Blumstein, P. W., Carssow, K. G., Hall, J., Hawkins, B., Hoffman, R., Ishem, E., Maurer, C. P., Spens, D., Taylor, J., & Zimmerman, D. L. (1974). The honoring of accounts. *American Sociological Review, 39,* 551–566.

Bochner, A. P. (1985). Perspectives on inquiry: Representation, conversation, and reflection. In M. L. Knapp & G. R. Miller (Eds.), *Handbook of interpersonal communication* (pp. 27–58). Beverly Hills, CA: Sage.

Bonner still riding high after Indy. (1992, June 7). *The Boston Sunday Globe,* p. 69.

Bowker, R. R. (1995). *34th Edition Ulrich's International Periodicals Directory 1996.* New Providence, NJ: Reed Reference.

Bradley, G. (1978). Self-serving biases in the attribution process: A re-examination of the fact or fiction question. *Journal of Personality and Social Psychology, 36,* 56–71.

Brannigan, A. (1981). *The social basis for scientific discoveries.* Cambridge: Cambridge University Press.

Brash on the Fourth of July. (1990, June 29/July 1). *USA Weekend,* p. 4.

Brehm, J. W., & Cole, A. H. (1966). Effect of a favor which reduces freedom. *Journal of Personality and Social Psychology, 3,* 420–426.

Bromley, D. B. (1993). *Reputation, image, and impression management.* Chichester, England: John Wiley and Sons.

Broverman, I. K., Vogel, S. R., Broverman, D. M., Clarkson, F. E., & Rosenkrantz, P. S. (1972). Sex-role stereotypes: A current appraisal. *Journal of Social Issues, 28,* 59–78.

Brown, J. D., & Gallagher, F. M. (1992). Coming to terms with failure: Private self-enhancement and public self-effacement. *Journal of Experimental Social Psychology, 28,* 3–22.

Brown, P., & Levinson, S. C. (1978). Universals in language usage: Politeness phenomena. In E. N. Goody (Ed.), *Questions and politeness: Strategies in social interaction* (pp. 56–289). Cambridge: Cambridge University Press.

————. (1987). *Universals in language usage: Politeness phenomena.* Cambridge: Cambridge University Press.

Brummett, B., & Duncan, M. C. (1992). Toward a discursive ontology of media. *Critical Studies in Mass Communication, 9,* 229–249.

Bruner, J. (1990). *Acts of meaning.* Cambridge, MA: Harvard University Press.

Bryant, J., Comisky, P., & Zillmann, D. (1977). Drama in sports commentary. *Journal of Communication, 27,* 140–149.

Bryne, D. (1961). Interpersonal attraction and attitude similarity. *Journal of Abnormal and Social Psychology, 62,* 713–715.

————. (1971). *The attraction paradigm.* New York: Academic Press.

Buttny, R. (1977). Sequence and practical reasoning in accounts episodes. *Communication Quarterly, 35,* 67–83.

————. (1993). *Social accountability in communication.* London: Sage.

Cameroon shocks Argentina. (1990, June 9). *Columbia Daily Tribune,* p. 11B.

Campbell, J. (1956). *Hero with a thousand faces.* New York: Bollingen.

Cards sidestep Mets' comeback. (1990, August 5). *Columbia Daily Tribune,* p. 13B.

Carruth, G. (1991). *What happened when.* New York: Penguin.

Cash, T. F., Gillen, B., & Burns, D. S. (1977). Sexism and "beautyism" in personnel consultant decision-making. *Journal of Applied Psychology, 62,* 301–310.

Cawelti, J. G. (1965). *Apostles of the self-made man.* Chicago: University of Chicago Press.

Cheek, J. M., & Hogan, R. (1983). Self-concepts, self-presentations, and moral judgments. In J. Suls & A. G. Greenwald (Eds.), *Psychological perspectives on the self* (Vol. 2, pp. 249–275). Hillsdale, NJ: Erlbaum.

Chenoweth, L. (1974). *The American dream of success.* North Scituate, MA: Duxbury Press.

Cheska, A. T. (1979). Sport spectacular: A ritual method of power. *International Review of Sports Sociology, 14*, 51–72.

Cialdini, R. B. (1989). Self-presentation by association. *Journal of Personality and Social Psychology, 57*, 626–631.

Cialdini, R. B., Borden, R. J., Thorne, A., Walker, M. R., Freeman, S., & Sloan, L. R. (1976). Basking in reflected glory: Three (football) field studies. *Journal of Personality and Social Psychology, 34*, 366–375.

Cody, M. J., & McLaughlin, M. L. (1985). Models for the sequential construction of accounting episodes: Situational and interactional constraints on message selection and evaluation. In R. L. Street & J. N. Capella (Eds.), *Sequence and pattern in communication behavior* (pp. 50–69). London: Edward Arnold.

Corliss, R. (1995, July 24). Hugh and cry: Two weeks after his arrest, Grant takes to the talk shows and the multiplexes. *Time, 146*, 58.

Craig, R. T., Tracy, K., & Spisak, F. (1986). The discourse of requests: Assessment of a politeness approach. *Human Communication Research, 12*, 437–468.

Croxton, J. S., & Klonsky, B. G. (1982). Sex differences in causal attributions for success and failure in real and hypothetical sport settings. *Sex Roles, 8*, 399–409.

Daintith, J., Egerton, H., Fergusson, R., Stibbs, A., & Wright, E. (Eds.) (1989). *The Macmillan dictionary of quotations.* New York: Macmillan.

Dallas defense steels show. (1996, January 29). *Columbia Daily Tribune*, p. 10B.

D'Arcy, E. (1963). *Human acts.* New York: Oxford University Press.

Dare to dream. (1993, June). *Applause*, 6–9.

Davis, K. E., & Florquist, C. C. (1965). Perceived threat and dependence as determinants of tactical usage of opinion conformity. *Journal of Experimental Social Psychology, 24*, 285–290.

Deaux, K. (1976). Sex: A perspective on the attribution process. In J. H. Harvey, W. J. Ickes, & R. F. Kidd (Eds.), *New directions in attribution research* (pp. 335–352). New York: Wiley & Sons.

Deaux, K., & Emswiller, T. (1974). Explanations of successful performance on sex-linked tasks: What is skill for the male is luck for the female. *Journal of Personality and Social Psychology, 29*, 80–85.

Deaux, K., & Farris, E. (1977). Attributing cause for one's performance: The effects of sex, norms, and outcome. *Journal of Research in Personality, 11*, 59–72.

Deaux, K., & Major, B. (1987). Putting gender into context: An interactive model of gender-related behavior. *Psychological Review, 94*, 369–389.

Deaux, K., & Taynor, J. (1973). Evaluation of male and female ability bias works two ways. *Psychological Reports, 32*, 261–262.

Decker, W. H. (1987). Attributions based on managers' self-presentation, sex, and weight. *Psychological Reports, 61*, 175–181.

————. (1990). Managing impressions of individual and group achievement through self-presentation. *Journal of Social Behavior and Personality*, 5, 287–296.

DePaulo, B. M. (1992). Nonverbal behavior and self-presentation. *Psychological Bulletin*, 111, 203–243.

Devers conquers all and captures the 100. (1992, August 2). *The New York Times*, p. 25.

Dickoff, H. (1964). Reactions to evaluations by another person as a function of self-evaluations and the interaction context. *Dissertation Abstracts International*, 24, 2166A.

Dipboye, R. L., & Wiley, J. W. (1977). Reactions of college recruiters to interviewee sex and self-presentation style. *Journal of Vocational Behavior*, 10, 1–12.

————. (1978). Reactions of male raters to interviewee self-presentation style and sex: Extensions of previous research. *Journal of Vocational Behavior*, 13, 192–203.

Discover for yourself. (1992, June). *Applause*, 1–6.

Dole, B. (1996). A personal message. Available from http://www.dole96.com/dole96/about/personal.html.

Drexler keeps his promise. (1990, June 8). *Columbia Daily Tribune*, p. 16B.

Duncan, M. C. & Brummett, B. (1991). The mediation of spectator sport. In L. Vande Berg & L. A. Wenner (Eds.), *Television criticism: Approaches and applications* (pp. 367–387). New York: Longman.

DuPlessis, R. B. (1985). *Writing beyond the ending*. Bloomington: Indiana University Press.

Eagly, A. H., & Acksen, B. A. (1971). The effect of expecting to be evaluated on change toward favorable and unfavorable information about oneself. *Sociometry*, 34, 411–422.

Edwards, H. (1973). *The sociology of sport*. Homewood, IL: Dorsey.

Etaugh, C., & Brown, B. (1975). Perceiving the causes of success and failure of male and female performers. *Developmental Psychology*, 11, 103.

Faces of the games. (1992, August 10). *Sports Illustrated*, 76, 92–99.

Farnham, A. (1993, September 20). Mary Kay's lessons in leadership. *Fortune*, 128, 68–71, 74, 76–77.

Feather, N. T., & Simon, J. G. (1975). Reactions to male and female success and failure in sex-linked occupations: Impressions of personality, causal attributions and perceived likelihood of different consequences. *Journal of Personality and Social Psychology*, 31, 20–31.

Figler, S. K., & Whitaker, G. (1991). *Sport and play in American life: A textbook in the sociology of sport*. Dubuque, IA: Wm. C. Brown.

Fine, G. A. (1978). Preadolescent socialization through organized athletics: The construction of moral meanings in Little League baseball. In M. Krotte (Ed.), *The dimensions of sport sociology* (pp. 79–105). West Point: Leisure Press.

Fisher, W. R. (1987). *Human communication as narrative: Toward a philosophy of reason, value, and action.* Columbia, SC: University of South Carolina Press.

Fletcher, C. (1990). The relationships between candidate personality, self-presentation styles, and interviewer assessments in selection interviews: An empirical study. *Human Relations, 43,* 739–749.

Former wrestler dives for Olympic gold. (1992, July 30). *Columbia Daily Tribune,* p. 3B.

Freccero, J. (1986). Autobiography and narrative. In T. C. Heller, M. Sosna, & D. E. Wellbery (Eds.), *Reconstructing individualism* (pp. 16–29). Stanford: Stanford University Press.

Frye, N. (1957). *Anatomy of criticism: Four essays.* Princeton, NJ: Princeton University Press.

Fucini, J. J., & Fucini, S. (1985). *Entrepreneurs: The men and women behind famous brand names and how they made it.* Boston: G. K. Hall.

Gene find aids search to cure Alzheimer's. (1995, June 28). *Columbia Daily Tribune,* p. 7A.

Gergen, K. J., & Gergen, M. M. (1988). Narrative and the self as relationship. In L. Berkowitz (Ed.), *Advances in experimental social psychology* (Vol. 21, pp. 17–56). San Diego, CA: Academic Press.

Gergen, K. J., & Wishnov, B. (1965). Others' self-evaluation and interaction anticipation as determinants of self-presentation. *Journal of Personality and Social Psychology, 2,* 348–358.

Gergen, M. (1992). Life stories: Pieces of a dream. In G. C. Rosenwald & R. L. Ochberg. (Eds.), *Storied lives: The cultural politics of self-understanding* (pp. 127–144). New Haven, CT: Yale University Press.

German lifter makes comeback complete. (1992, August 4). *Chicago Tribune,* Sec. 4, p. 7.

Giacalone, R. A. (1985). On slipping when you thought you had put your best foot forward: Self-promotion, self-destruction and entitlements. *Group and Organizational Studies, 10,* 61–80.

Giacalone, R. A., & Riordan, C. A. (1990). Effect of self-presentation on perceptions and recognition in an organization. *Journal of Psychology, 124,* 25–38.

Giacalone, R. A., & Rosenfeld, P. (1984). The effect of perceived planning and propriety on the effectiveness of leadership accounts. *Social Behavior and Personality, 12,* 217–224.

Gilbert overtakes Snead in Kroger Senior Classic. (1992, July 5). *Columbia Daily Tribune,* p. 3B.

Glaser, B. (1978). *Theoretical sensitivity.* Mill Valley, CA: Sociology Press.

Glaser, B., & Strauss, A. (1967). *The discovery of grounded theory: Strategies for qualitative research.* Chicago: Aldine.

Godfrey, D. K., Jones, E. E., & Lord, C. G. (1986). Self-promotion is not ingratiating. *Journal of Personality and Social Psychology, 50,* 106–115.

Goffman, E. (1959). *The presentation of self in everyday life*. Garden City, NY: Doubleday.

———. (1967). *Interaction ritual*. Garden City, NY: Doubleday Anchor.

———. (1971). *Relations in public*. New York: Basic Books.

Goldlust, J. (1987). *Playing for keeps: Sport, the media, and society*. Melbourne, Australia: Longman Cheshire.

Goldstein, J., & Smucker, J. (1986). Multitracking: The success ethic in an era of diminished opportunities. *Youth and Society, 18*, 127–149.

Gonzales, M. H., Pederson, J. H., Manning, D. J., & Wetter, D. W. (1990). Pardon my gaffe: Effects of sex, status, and consequence severity on accounts. *Journal of Personality and Social Psychology, 58*, 610–621.

Goode, W. J. (1978). *The celebration of heroes: Prestige as a social control system*. Berkeley: University of California Press.

Gouldner, A. (1960). The norm of reciprocity. *American Sociological Review, 25*, 161–178.

Guinness Multimedia Disc of Records. (1995). [CD-ROM]. Danbury, CT: Grolier Electronic Publishing.

Hale, C. L. (1986). Impact of cognitive complexity on message structure in a face-threatening context. *Journal of Language and Social Psychology, 5*, 135–143.

———. (1987). A comparison of accounts: When is a failure not a failure? *Journal of Language and Social Psychology, 6*, 117–132.

Hardesty, S., & Jacobs, N. (1986). *Success and betrayal: The crisis of women in corporate America*. New York: Franklin Watts.

Harris, D. (1995, January). 16th annual salary survey: 1995. *Working Woman, 20*, 25.

Harris, D. V., & Harris, B. L. (1984). *The athlete's guide to sports psychology: Mental skills for physical people*. New York: Leisure Press.

Heider, F. (1958). *The psychology of interpersonal relations*. New York: Wiley.

Heilman, M. E., & Guzzo, R. A. (1978). The perceived cause of work success as a mediator of sex discrimination in organizations. *Organizational Behavior and Human Performance, 21*, 346–357.

Henderson shifts into third to pass Cobb. (1990, May 30). *Columbia Daily Tribune*, p. 11B.

Hennig, M., & Jardim, A. (1977). *The managerial woman*. New York: Pocket Books.

Herzberg, F. (1959). *The motivation to work* (2nd ed.). New York: Wiley.

Hogan, R., Jones, W. H., & Cheek, J. M. (1985). Socioanalytic theory: An alternative to armadillo psychology. In B. R. Schlenker (Ed.), *The self and social life* (pp. 175–198). New York: McGraw Hill.

Holtgraves, T. (1989). The form and function of remedial moves: Reported use, psychological reality, and perceived effectiveness. *Journal of Language and Social Psychology, 8*, 1–16.

————. (1992). The linguistic realization of face management: Implications for language production and comprehension, person perception, and cross-cultural communication. *Social Psychology Quarterly, 55,* 141–159.

Holtgraves, T., & Srull, T. K. (1989). The effects of positive self-descriptions on impressions: General principles and individual differences. *Personality and Social Psychology Bulletin, 15,* 452–462.

House, W. C. (1980). Effects of knowledge that attributions will be observed by others. *Journal of Research in Personality, 14,* 528–545.

Huber, R. M. (1971). *The American idea of success.* New York: McGraw Hill.

Hyman, R. (1985). *Dictionary of quotations.* Lincolnwood, IL: National Textbook Company.

Innes, J. M., Dormer, S., & Lukins, J. (1993). Knowledge of gender stereotypes and attitudes towards women: A preliminary report. *Psychological Reports, 73,* 1005–1006.

In the pink: Mary Kay celebrates 30 years. (1993, September 19). *St. Louis Post Dispatch,* p. 1E.

Irwin goes overtime for U.S. Open title. (1990, June 19). *Columbia Daily Tribune,* p. 11B.

Iso-Ahola, S. E. (1975). A test of attribution theory of success and failure with Little League baseball players. *Movement, 7,* 323–337.

Jackson, D. D. (1988, November). While he expected the worst, Nobel hoped for the best. *Smithsonian, 19,* 201.

Jacobs, S. (1988). Evidence and inference in conversation analysis. In J. Anderson (Ed.), *Communication yearbook 11* (pp. 433–443). Newbury Park, CA: Sage.

Jazzy Harry. (1990, July 6–8). *USA Weekend,* p. 5.

Jelinek, E. (1980). *Women's autobiography: Essays in criticism.* Bloomington, IN: Indiana University Press.

Jellison, J. M. (1990). Accounting: Societal implications. In M. J. Cody & M. L. McLaughlin (Eds.), *The psychology of tactical communication* (pp. 283–298). Clevedon: Multilingual Matters.

Jellison, J. M., & Gentry, K. A. (1978). Self-presentation interpretations of the seeking of social approval. *Personality and Social Psychology Bulletin, 4,* 227–230.

Jhally, S. (1989). Cultural studies and the sports/media complex. In L. A. Wenner (Ed.), *Media, sports, and society* (pp. 204–224). Newbury Park, CA: Sage.

Jones, E. E. (1964). *Ingratiation: A social psychological analysis.* New York: Appleton.

————. (1965). Conformity as a tactic of ingratiation. *Science, 149,* 144–150.

Jones, E. E., Gergen, K. G., & Jones, R. G. (1963). Tactics of ingratiation among leaders and subordinates in a status hierarchy. *Psychological Monographs, 77,* (3, Whole No. 566), 1–20.

Jones, E. E., Jones, R. G., & Gergen, K. G. (1963). Some conditions affecting the evaluation of a conformist. *Journal of Personality, 31,* 270–288.

Jones, E. E. & Pittman, T. S. (1980). Toward a general theory of strategic self-presentation. In J. Suls & A. G. Greenwald (Eds.), *Psychological perspectives on the self* (Vol. 2, pp. 231–262). Hillsdale, NJ: Erlbaum.

Jones, E. E., & Schneider, D. J. (1968). Certainty of self-appraisal and reactions to evaluations from others. *Sociometry, 31,* 395–403.

Jones, E. E., & Wortman, C. (1973). *Ingratiation: An attributional approach.* Morristown, NJ: General Learning Press.

Kanouse, D. E., Gumpert, P., & Canavan-Gumpert, D. (1981). The semantics of praise. In J. H. Harvey, W. I. Ickes, & R. I. Kidd (Eds.), *New directions in attribution research* (Vol. 3, pp. 97–115). Hillsdale, NJ: Erlbaum.

Kauffman, D. R., & Skiner, J. D. (1968). Conformity as an ingratiation technique. *Journal of Experimental and Social Psychology, 4,* 400–414.

KC downs Raiders for division lead. (1990, November 26). *Columbia Daily Tribune,* p. 11B.

Kellerman, K. (1992). Communication: Inherently strategic and primarily automatic. *Communication Monographs, 59,* 288–300.

Kipnis, D., & Vanderveer, R. (1971). Ingratiation and the use of power. *Journal of Personality and Social Psychology, 17,* 280–286.

Klein, F. C. (1979, June 26). The press' cozy relationship with sports. *The Wall Street Journal,* p. 18.

Kline, S. L. (1985). Social cognitive determinants of face support in persuasive messages. *Dissertation Abstracts International, 45,* 3238–3239A.

Knorr-Cetina, K. (1981). *The manufacture of knowledge.* Oxford: Pergamon Press.

Latour, B., & Woolgar, S. (1979). *Laboratory life: The social construction of scientific facts.* London: Sage.

Lau, R. R. (1984). Dynamics of the attribution process. *Journal of Personality and Social Psychology, 46,* 1017–1028.

Lau, R. R., & Russell, D. (1980). Attributions in the sports pages. *Journal of Personality and Social Psychology, 39,* 29–38.

Leary, M. R. (1992). Self-presentational processes in exercise and sport. *Journal of Sport and Exercise Psychology, 14,* 339–351.

Leary, M. R., & Kowalski, R. M. (1990). Impression management: A literature review and two-component model. *Psychological Bulletin, 107,* 34–47.

Leith, L. M. (1989). Causal attributions and sports behavior: Implications for practitioners. *Journal of Sport Behavior, 12,* 213–225.

Lidz, F. (1992, July 22). Hot shots. *Sports Illustrated, 76,* 92–93.

Lipsky, R. (1975). *Sports world: An American dreamland.* New York: Quadrangle.

————. (1978). Toward a political theory of American sports symbolism. *American Behavioral Scientist, 21,* 345–360.

Long, E. (1981). Affluence and after: Themes of success in American best-selling novels, 1945–1975. In R. A. Jones & H. Kuklick (Eds.), *Knowledge and society: Studies in the sociology of culture past and present* (Vol. 3, pp. 257–301). Greenwich, CT: JAI Press.

Long wait finally rewarding. (1992, August 3). *Columbia Daily Tribune,* p. 10B.

Lucky find? (1996, January 24). *Columbia Daily Tribune,* p. 4A.

Macksey, J., & Macksey, K. (1975). *The book of women's achievements.* New York: Stein and Day.

Magrane, two relievers, help Cardinals break Mets' streak. (1990, September 5). *Columbia Daily Tribune,* p. 13B.

Mandlebaum, J., & Pomerantz, A. (1991). What drives social action? In K. Tracy (Ed.), *Understanding face-to-face interaction: Issues linking goals and discourse* (pp. 131–150). Hillsdale, NJ: Erlbaum.

Mark, M. M., Mutrie, N., Brooks, D. R., & Harris, D. V. (1984). Causal attributions of winners and losers in individual competitive sports: Toward a reformulation of the self-serving bias. *Journal of Sport Psychology, 6,* 184–196.

Martinko, M. J., Weiner, B., & Lord, R. G. (Ed.). (1995). *Attribution theory: An organizational perspective.* Delray Beach, FL: St. Lucie Press.

Maslow, A. H. (1970). *Motivation and personality* (2nd ed.). New York: Free Press.

McCain, G., & Segal, E. M. (1982). *The game of science* (4th ed.). Monterey, CA: Brooks/Cole.

McGee boosts average, team against Cubs. (1990, August 10). *Columbia Daily Tribune,* p. 13B.

McLaughlin, M. L., Cody, M. J., & Rosenstein, N. E. (1983). Account sequences in conversations between strangers. *Communication Monographs, 50,* 102–125.

Merton, R. K. (1957a). Priorities in scientific discovery: A chapter in the sociology of science. *American Sociological Review, 22,* 635–659.

————. (1957b). *Social theory and social structure.* New York: Free Press.

Mette, D. R. (1971). Changes in liking as a function of the magnitude and affect of sequential evaluations. *Journal of Experimental Social Psychology, 7,* 157–172.

Metts, S., & Cupach, W. R. (1989). Situational influence on the use of remedial strategies in embarrassing predicaments. *Communication Monographs, 56,* 151–162.

Mieder, W., Kingsbury, S. A., & Harder, K. B. (Eds.). (1992). *A dictionary of American proverbs.* Oxford: Oxford University Press.

Miller, D. T., & Ross, M. (1975). Self-serving biases in the attribution of causality: Fact or fiction? *Psychological Bulletin, 82,* 213–225.

Miller, L. C., Cooke, L. L., Tsang, J., & Morgan, F. (1992). Should I brag? Nature and impact of positive and boastful disclosures for women and men. *Human Communication Research*, *18*, 364–399.

Muir, D., & Weinstein, E. (1962). The social debt: An investigation of lower-class and middle-class norms of social obligation. *American Sociological Review*, *27*, 532–539.

Mulgannon, T. (1992, June). Merely perfect. *Sport*, *83*, 55–56.

Mulkay, M. (1984). The ultimate compliment: A sociological analysis of ceremonial discourse. *Sociology*, *18*, 531–549.

Murphy, A. (1992, July 22). Head-to-head: Kieren Perkins vs. Jorg Hoffman. *Sports Illustrated*, *76*, 66.

Navratilova moves on; Gomez ousted. (1990, August 30). *Columbia Daily Tribune*, p. 15B.

Navratilova slams Garrison. (1990, July 8). *Columbia Daily Tribune*, p. 13B.

Nelan, B. (1994, July 4). As the plutonium cools. *Time*, *144*, 33.

Nelson, M. (1980). Feminism, the jockocracy, and men's liberation: Crying all the way to the bank. In D. F. Sabo & R. Runfola (Eds.), *Jock: Sports and male identity* (pp. 239–248). Englewood Cliffs, NJ: Prentice-Hall.

Nightingale, D. (1992, March 2). Saving grace. *The Sporting News*, p. 13.

Nixon, H. L. (1984). *Sport and the American dream*. New York: Leisure Press.

Nobel Foundation. *Les Prix Nobel en 1967*. Stockholm: Imprimerie Royale P. A. Norstedt & Söner.

Nobel Foundation. *Les Prix Nobel en 1987*. Stockholm: Imprimerie Royale P. A. Norstedt & Söner.

Nobel Foundation. *Les Prix Nobel en 1988*. Stockholm: Imprimerie Royale P. A. Norstedt & Söner.

Nobel Foundation. *Les Prix Nobel en 1989*. Stockholm: Imprimerie Royale P. A. Norstedt & Söner.

NSD debut: A fortune cookie sealed her fate. (1993, June). *Applause*, 27.

Oestreich, J. R. (1995, August 15). Andre Watts. *The New York Times*, *144*, p. B3.

O'Keefe, B. J. (1988). The logic of message design: Individual differences in reasoning about communication. *Communication Monographs*, *55*, 80–103.

———. (1991). Message design logic and the management of multiple goals. In K. Tracy (Ed.), *Understanding face-to-face interaction: Issues linking goals and discourse* (pp. 131–150). Hillsdale, NJ: Lawrence Erlbaum.

O'Keefe, B. J., & Shepherd, G. J. (1987). The pursuit of multiple objectives in face-to-face persuasive interactions: Effects of construct differentiation on message production. *Communication Monographs*, *54*, 396–419.

———. (1989). The communication of identity during face-to-face persuasive interactions: Effects of perceiver's construct differentiation and target's message strategies. *Communication Research*, *16*, 375–404.

Phillip, M. C. (1995, March 9). Between laughter and tears: An expurgated Maya Angelou on stage. *Black Issues in Higher Education, 12,* 1–3.

Pirates beat Cards, clinch East. (1990, October 1). *Columbia Daily Tribune,* p. 9B.

Pomerantz, A. (1978). Compliment responses: Notes on the co-operation of multiple constraints. In J. Schenkein (Ed.), *Studies in the organization of conversational interaction* (pp. 79–112). New York: Academic Press.

President brags about economy. (1994, February 14). *Columbia Daily Tribune,* p. 10A.

Putting record inconsequential to leader. (1992, July 11). *Columbia Daily Tribune,* p. 2B.

Ralston, D. A., & Elsass, P. M. (1991). Conformity: A subtle means of impression management. In R. A. Giacalone & P. Rosenfeld (Eds.), *Applied impression management: How image-making affects managerial decisions* (pp. 241–258). Newbury Park, CA: Sage.

Reader's Digest. (1975). *The Reader's Digest treasury of modern quotations.* New York: Thomas Y. Crowell Co.

Red Sox defeat ghosts. (1990, October 4). *Columbia Daily Tribune,* p. 17B.

Regan, J. W. (1976). Liking for evaluators: Consistency and self-esteem theories. *Journal of Experimental Social Psychology, 12,* 156–169.

Reis, W. T., & Gruzen, J. (1976). On mediating equity, equality and self-interest: The role of self-presentation in social exchange. *Journal of Experimental Social Psychology, 12,* 487–503.

Retired, Colin Powell. (1993, October 11). *Time, 142,* 25.

Riger, S., & Galligan, P. (1980). Women in management: An exploration of composing paradigms. *American Psychologist, 42,* 104–106.

Riordan, C. A., & Marlin, N. A. (1987). Some good news about bad practices. *American Psychologist, 42,* 104–106.

Riordan, C. A., Marlin, N.A., & Gidwani, K. (1988). Accounts offered for unethical research practices: Effects on the evaluation of acts and actors. *The Journal of Social Psychology, 128,* 495–505.

Riordan, C. A., Marlin, N. A., & Kellogg, R. T. (1983). The effectiveness of accounts following transgression. *Social Psychology Quarterly, 46,* 213–219.

Riordan, C. A., Thomas, J. S., & James, M. K. (1985). Attributions in a one-on-one sports competition: Evidence for self-serving biases and gender differences. *Journal of Sport Behavior, 8,* 42–53.

Rockman, J. (1980, July). Door-to-door dollars. *Working Woman, 5,* 36–38, 76.

Rokeach, M. (1973). *The nature of human values.* New York: Wiley.

Rolling in dough. (1995, July 5). *Columbia Daily Tribune,* p. 12A.

Roloff, M. E. (1981). *Interpersonal communication: The social exchange approach.* Beverly Hills, CA: Sage.

Rosenwald, G. C., & Ochberg, R. L. (1992). *Storied lives: The cultural politics of self-understanding.* New Haven, CT: Yale University Press.

Roth, P. (1973). *The great American novel.* New York: Bantam.

Russ, J. (1972). What can a heroine do? Or why women can't write. In S. Koppelman Cornillion (Ed.), *Images of women in fiction: Feminist perspectives* (pp. 3–20). Bowling Green: Bowling Green University Popular Press.

Rypien's truth hurts Buffalo. (1992, January 27). *Columbia Daily Tribune*, p. 1B.

Saberhagen loses another pitchers' duel. (1990, June 23). *Columbia Daily Tribune*, p. 13B.

Sampras makes U.S. Open history. (1990, September 10). *Columbia Daily Tribune*, p. 9B.

Schlenker, B. R. (1980). *Impression management: The self-concept, social identity, and interpersonal relations.* Monterey, CA: Brooks/Cole.

———. (1982). Translating actions into attitudes: An identity-analytic approach to the explanation of social conduct. In L. Berkowitz (Ed.) *Advances in experimental social psychology.* (Vol. 15, pp. 194–247). New York: Academic Press.

———. (Ed.) (1985). *The self and social life.* New York: McGraw Hill.

———. (1986). Self-identification: Toward an integration of the private and public self. In R. F. Baumeister (Ed.), *Public self and private self* (pp. 21–62). New York: Springer-Verlag.

Schlenker, B. R., & Darby, B. W. (1981). The use of apologies in social predicaments. *Social Psychology Quarterly, 44,* 271–278.

Schlenker, B. R., & Leary, M. R. (1982). Audiences' reactions to self-enhancing, self-denigrating, and accurate self-presentations. *Journal of Experimental and Social Psychology, 18,* 89–104.

Schlenker, B. R., & Wiegold, M. F. (1990). Self-consciousness and self-presentation: Being autonomous versus appearing autonomous. *Journal of Personality and Social Psychology, 59,* 820–828.

———. (1992). Interpersonal processes involving impression regulation and management. In M. R. Rosenzweig & L. M. Porter (Eds.), *Annual Review of Psychology* (Vol. 43, pp. 133–168). Palo Alto, CA: Annual Reviews.

Schlenker, B. R., Wiegold, M. F., & Hallam, J. R. (1990). Self-serving attributions in social context: Effects of self-esteem and social pressure. *Journal of Experimental and Social Psychology, 58,* 855–863.

Schlessinger, B. S., & Schlessinger, J. H. (Eds.) (1991). *The who's who of Nobel Prize winners 1901–1990* (2nd ed.). Phoenix, AZ: Oryx Press.

Schneider, D. J. (1969). Tactical self-presentation after success and failure. *Journal of Personality and Social Psychology, 13,* 262–268.

———. (1981). Tactical self-presentations: Toward a broader conception. In J. T. Tedeschi (Ed.), *Impression management theory and social psychological research* (pp. 23–39). New York: Academic Press.

Schneider, D. J., & Eustis, A. C. (1972). Effects of ingratiation motivation, target positiveness, and revealingness on self-presentation. *Journal of Personality and Social Psychology, 22,* 149–155.

Schönbach, P. (1980). A category system for account phases. *European Journal of Social Psychology, 10,* 195–200.

————. (1990). *Account episodes: The management or escalation of conflict.* Cambridge: Cambridge University Press.

Schopler, J., & Thompson, V. D. (1968). Role of attribution processes in mediating amount of reciprocity for a favor. *Journal of Personality, 10,* 243–250.

Scott, M. B., & Lyman, S. M. (1968). Accounts. *American Sociological Review, 33,* 46–62.

Semin, G. R., & Manstead, A. S. R. (1983). *The accountability of conduct: A social psychological analysis.* London: Academic Press.

Six, B., & Eckes, T. (1991). A closer look at the complex structure of gender stereotypes. *Sex Roles, 24,* 57–71.

Slugoski, B. R., & Ginsburg, G. P. (1989). Ego identity and explanatory speech. In J. Shotter & K. J. Gergen (Eds.), *Texts of identity* (pp. 36–55). London: Sage.

Smoking the field. (1992, July 13). *Columbia Daily Tribune,* p. 10B.

Snyder, C. R., Higgins, R. L., & Stucky, R. J. (1983). *Excuses: Masquerades in search of grace.* New York: John Wiley.

Snyder, E. E. (1972). Athletic dressing room slogans as folklore: A means of socialization. *International Review of Sport Sociology, 7,* 89–102.

Snyder, E. E., & Spreitzer, E. A. (1978). *Social aspects of sport* (2nd ed.). Englewood Cliffs, NJ: Prentice-Hall.

Snyder, M. L., Stephan, W. G., & Rosenfield, D. (1978). Attributional egotism. In J. Harvey, W. Ickes, & R. Kidd (Eds.), *New directions in attribution research* (Vol. 2, pp. 91–117). Hillsdale, NJ: Erlbaum.

Sprinter completes comeback. (1992, June 21). *Columbia Daily Tribune,* p. 1B.

Steele, E. D., & Redding, W. C. (1962). The American value system: Premises for persuasion. *Western Speech, 26,* 83–91.

Steinberg, J. (1984). *Climbing the ladder of success in highheels.* Ann Arbor, MI: UMI Research Press.

Strauss, A. L. (1990). *Qualitative analysis for social scientists* (4th ed.). Cambridge: Cambridge University Press.

Summit set to sign START II. (1992, December 30). *Columbia Daily Tribune,* p. 1A.

Sykes, G. M., & Matza, D. (1957). Techniques of neutralization: A theory of delinquency. *American Sociological Review, 22,* 664–670.

Taylor, D. M., & Doria, J. R. (1981). Self-serving and group-serving bias in attribution. *The Journal of Social Psychology, 113,* 201–211.

Tedeschi, J. T., & Linkskold, S. (1976). *Social psychology: Interdependence, interaction and influence.* New York: Wiley.

Tedeschi, J. T., & Melburg, V. (1984). Impression management and influence in the organization. In S. B. Bacharach & E. J. Lawler (Eds.), *Research in the sociology of organizations* (Vol. 3, pp. 31–58). Greenwich, CT: JAI Press.

Tedeschi, J. T., & Norman, N. (1985). Social power, self-presentation, and the self. In B. R. Schlenker (Ed.), *The self and social life* (pp. 293–322). New York: McGraw Hill.

Tedeschi, J. T., & Riess, M. (1981a). Identities, the phenomenal self, and laboratory research. In J. T. Tedeschi (Ed.) *Impression management theory and social psychological research* (pp. 3–22). New York: Academic Press.

———. (1981b). Verbal strategies in impression management. In C. Antaki (Ed.), *The psychology of ordinary explanations of social behaviour* (pp. 271–309). New York: Academic Press.

Tesser, A., Gatewood, R., & Driver, M. (1968). Some determinants of gratitude. *Journal of Personality and Social Psychology, 9,* 233–236.

Tetlock, P. E., & Manstead, A. R. S. (1985). Impression management versus intrapsychic explanations in social psychology: A useful dichotomy? *Psychological Review, 92,* 59–77.

They said it. (1993, May 31). *Sports Illustrated, 77,* 16.

Thibaut, J. W., & Kelley, H. H. (1978). *Interpersonal relations: A theory of interdependence.* New York: Wiley.

30 years of dreams come true. (1993, September). *Applause,* 6.

Tracy, K. (1990). The many faces of facework. In H. Giles & P. Robinson (Eds.), *Handbook of language and social psychology* (pp. 209–226). London: Wiley.

Tracy, K., & Baratz, S. (1995). Intellectual discussion in the academy as situated discourse. *Communication Monographs, 60,* 300–320.

Tracy, K., & Coupland, N. (1990). Multiple goals in discourse: An overview of issues. *Journal of Language and Social Psychology, 9,* 1–13.

Tracy, K., & Naughton, J. (1994). The identity work of questioning in intellectual discussion. *Communication Monographs, 61,* 281–302.

Trujillo, N. (1991). Hegemonic masculinity on the mound: Media representations of Nolan Ryan and American sports culture. *Critical Studies in Mass Communication, 8,* 209–308.

———. (1992). Interpreting (the work and the talk of) baseball: Perspectives on ballpark culture. *Western Journal of Communication, 56,* 350–371.

Trujillo, N., & Ekdom, L. R. (1985). Sportswriting and American cultural values: The 1984 Chicago Cubs. *Critical Studies in Mass Communication, 2,* 262–281.

U.S. struts golden stuff in sprints. (1992, August 6). *Columbia Daily Tribune,* p. 1B.

Vande Berg, L. R., & Trujillo, N. (1989). The rhetoric of winning and losing: The American dream and America's team. In L. A. Wenner (Ed.), *Media, sports, and society* (pp. 204–224). Newbury Park, CA: Sage.

Vander Velden, L. (1986). Heroes and bad winners: Cultural differences. In L. Vander Velden & J. H. Humphrey (Eds.), *Psychology and sociology of sport: Current selected research* (Vol. 1, pp. 205–220). New York: AMS Press.

Vecsey, G. (1983, March 16). A nation of sports fans. *The New York Times*, p. B11.

Veteran wins 10-meter event. (1992, June 21). *Columbia Daily Tribune*, p. 7B.

Waggoner, C. E. (1994). The nature and function of aesthetic communication in traditional women's cultures. Unpublished doctoral dissertation, The Ohio State University. *Dissertation Abstracts International*, *55*, 1421–1422A.

Weary, G., & Arkin, R. M. (1981). Attributional self-presentation. In J. H. Harvey, W. J. Ickes, & R. I. Kidd (Eds.), *New directions in attribution research* (Vol. 3, pp. 223–246). Hillsdale, NJ: Erlbaum.

Weiner, B. (1979). A theory of motivation for some classroom experiences. *Journal of Educational Psychology*, *71*, 3–25.

———. (1986). *An attributional theory of motivation and emotion*. New York: Springer-Verlag.

Weiner, B., Amirkhan, J., Folkes, F. S., & Verette, J. A. (1987). An attributional analysis of excuse-giving: Studies of a naive theory of emotion. *Journal of Personality and Social Psychology*, *52*, 316–324.

Welch clinches AL Cy Young. (1990, November 14). *Columbia Daily Tribune*, p. 15B.

Wenner, L. A. (1989). Media, sports, and society: The research agenda. In L. A. Wenner (Ed.), *Media, sports, and society* (pp. 204–224). Newbury Park, CA: Sage.

Whitehead, G. I., & Smith, S. H. (1986). Competence and excuse-making as self-presentational strategies. In R. F. Baumeister (Ed.), *Public self and private self* (pp. 161–177). New York: Springer-Verlag.

Whitson, D. (1990). Sport in the social construction of masculinity. In M. A. Messner & D. F. Sabo (Eds.), *Sport, men, and the gender order: Critical feminist perspectives* (pp. 19–29). Champaign, IL: Human Kinetics.

Wilhelm, P. (1983). *The Nobel Prize*. London: Springwood.

Williams, R. (1970). *American society*. New York: Alfred A. Knopf.

Wortman, C. B., & Linsenmeier, J. A. (1977). Interpersonal attraction and techniques of ingratiation in organizational settings. In B. M. Shaw & G. R. Salancik (Eds.), *New directions in organizational behavior* (pp. 133–178). Chicago: St. Clair Press.

Wyllie, I. (1954). *The self-made man in America*. New York: Free Press.

Zaccaro, S. J., Peterson, C., & Walker, S. (1987). Self-serving attributions for individual and group performance. *Social Psychology Quarterly*, *50*, 257–263.

Zientek, C. E. C., & Breakwell, G. M. (1991). Attributional schema of players before and after knowledge of game outcome. *Journal of Sport Behavior*, *14*, 211–220.

Zuckerman, H. (1977). *Scientific elite: Nobel laureates in the United States*. New York: Free Press.

Index